The Story of the
SECRET SERVICE

By HARRY EDWARD NEAL

GROSSET & DUNLAP • Publishers • New York

A National General Company

PICTURE ACKNOWLEDGMENTS
Wide World Photos: Pages 10, 13, 18, 19, 23, 103
All other photographs furnished by the Visual
Intelligence Branch, U.S. Secret Service.

Library of Congress Catalog Card Number: 70-106318

ISBN: 0-448-02655-4 (Trade Edition)
ISBN: 0-448-04289-4 (Library Edition)

Copyright © 1971 by Harry Edward Neal.
All rights reserved under International and Pan-American Copyright Conventions.
Published simultaneously in Canada.   Printed in the United States of America.

FOREWORD

I spent thirty-one years in the United States Secret Service. I began in New York City as a stenographer in 1926. I was commissioned as a Secret Service Agent in 1931. In 1940, when I was serving as Assistant Special Agent in Charge in the New York District, I was transferred to Washington as a member of the Chief's staff. A little later I became Executive Aide to the Chief, and in 1956 was appointed Assistant Chief. I elected to retire in 1957 to devote my full time to free-lance writing, which I now do.

I believe that no book, however long, could tell the full and complete story of the Secret Service—its ups and downs, the failures and triumphs of its agents, the drama, the comedy, the tragedy, the adventure found in its eternal fight against crime and in its security work.

Much of this personal kind of history never finds its way into official reports, much less into books. Instead, it often lies stored within hearts and heads, to be dredged up as audible memories in gatherings of old friends who look back proudly to exciting days and nights they will never see again.

However, I have tried here to tell the story of the Secret Service in such a way that the reader, hopefully, will understand the importance of the Secret Service role in our national affairs, and the reasons why members of the Service, active or retired, take justifiable pride in its achievements and traditions, and in the contributions these men and women have made to the building of one of the world's finest law-enforcement agencies.

I could not have written this book without the very generous and willing help of Secret Service personnel. For this cooperation I am deeply indebted to my old friend, Director James J. Rowley, to John W. Warner, Jr., Assistant to the Director, and to my good friend and former associate, A. E. Whitaker, Special Agent in Charge of the New York District.

I am especially grateful to Special Agent David Noznesky of Mr. Warner's staff, whose enthusiasm for the project equalled my own, and who helped immeasurably, even in the midst of his other and more important duties.

I hope that you will find my book both enjoyable and informative.

Harry Edward Neal

Assistant Chief,
U.S. Secret Service (Ret.)

Dedicated with affection and esteem
to the Special Agents of the United
States Secret Service, active and
retired, as a tribute to their
courage and devotion to duty.

CONTENTS

Chapter		Page
1	Dallas	11
2	The Secret Service Begins	16
3	Crackdown	21
4	The Bogus Bill Business	27
5	Undercover Agent	32
6	The Coiners	37
7	Bad Money Looks Bad	41
8	Lies for Loot	46
9	The Check Thieves	50
10	The Forged Bond Racket	55
11	The Secret Service Agent	59
12	Mission: Protection	69
13	Guardians in Uniform	81
14	Don't Make Death Threats	88
15	The Ninhydrin Trap	95
16	Modern Musketeers	101
17	Leaders and Laurels	107
	Index	123

Moving through the streets of Dallas, Texas, the open Presidential limousine carrying U.S. President John F. Kennedy and the First Lady, and the then Governor of Texas, John B. Connally, with his wife, prepares to turn a fateful corner. The time is midday, November 22, 1963. Less than a minute later, shots from an assassin's high-powered rifle were aimed at the Chief Executive with all-too-deadly accuracy.

Chapter 1

DALLAS

President John F. Kennedy and his wife, Jacqueline, sat comfortably in the back seat of their open Lincoln limousine, waving and smiling at crowds of people along the sidewalks in Dallas, Texas. It was about noontime on Friday, November 22, 1963, and skies that were cloudy earlier that morning were clearing.

The President and First Lady were on their way to a luncheon at the Trade Mart as the guests of Dallas business and civic leaders. They seemed pleased by the cheering and applause of the crowds. They could not know that very soon a man with a rifle would shoot and kill the President.

With them in the car, sitting on "jump seats," were John B. Connally, Jr., Governor of Texas, and his wife. The limousine was driven by Special Agent William R. Greer of the United States Secret Service. Next to him sat Roy H. Kellerman, another Special Agent.

A few feet behind the President's automobile was a "follow-up" open Cadillac with eight Secret Service men—two in the front seat, two in the rear, and two standing on each running board. (Running boards are not seen on today's automobiles, but are special equipment on the Secret Service vehicles used in Presidential parades and motorcades.)

Behind the follow-up Cadillac was another car occupied by Vice-President and Mrs. Lyndon B. Johnson, Senator Ralph W. Yarborough of Texas, Special Agent Rufus W. Youngblood of the Secret Service, and the driver.

More automobiles with luncheon guests made up the rest of the motorcade.

Twice along the way the President ordered his Secret Service driver to stop so that he might shake hands with people in the crowds. At each stop the Secret Service agents from the follow-up car ran forward and stood close to the President and Mrs. Kennedy.

It was about half-past twelve when the President's limousine turned off Houston Street into Elm Street, traveling at about eleven miles an hour. A Secret Service agent in the follow-up car sent word to the Trade Mart by radio that the Presidential party would arrive within another five minutes.

Seconds after this message was sent came the *crack! crack!* of rifle shots. (Later there were questions as to whether two or more shots were fired.) The President seized his neck with his hands. His body seemed to stiffen and he leaned forward for a moment, then fell sideways into Mrs. Kennedy's lap. He had been shot in the neck and head.

Secret Service Agent Clint Hill, riding in the follow-up car, had heard what sounded like a firecracker. Then he saw the President fall. Hill jumped to the pavement and ran forward to the limousine. Mrs. Kennedy was apparently trying to climb out of the back of the car. Hill leaped up, pushed her back, and kept her from falling into the street. Later Agent Hill said:

> "Mrs. Kennedy had jumped up from the seat and was, it appeared to me, reaching for something coming off the right rear bumper of the car, the right rear tail, when she noticed that I was trying to climb on the car. She turned toward me and I grabbed her and put her back in the back seat, then crawled up on top of the back seat and lay there."

One witness said that Mrs. Kennedy would probably have tumbled to the road and might have been killed if Agent Hill had not pushed her back into the seat. Mrs. Kennedy herself said she did not remember climbing onto the back of the car.

Many other things happened within a few seconds from the time the shots were fired. In Vice-President Johnson's car, Special Agent Youngblood heard the explosions and saw the quick movements of people near the President's car. Immediately he thought that shots might also be aimed at the Vice-President.

"I turned around, hit the Vice-President on the shoulder and hollered, 'Get down!'" he recalled. "Then I looked around again and saw more of this movement, so I climbed over to the back seat and got on top of him." In other words, Agent Youngblood shielded Mr. Johnson with his body.

Led by police escort, the limousine speeds to Parkland Hospital, but the shots have been fatal to the President. Secret Service Agent Clint Hill, making his way to the back seat, restrains Jacqueline Kennedy, seen standing.

In the President's car, Governor Connally was also seriously wounded. Agent Roy Kellerman, in the front seat, grabbed his microphone and radioed the police escort leading the motorcade. "We're hit!" he cried. "Get us to the hospital immediately!"

The full impact of the dreadful situation suddenly made itself felt. Governor Connally moaned, "Oh, no, no, no! My God! . . ."

He was lying with his head on his wife's lap. Mrs. Connally said, "It's all right. Be still."

With police sirens screaming, the cars raced at speeds of 70 to 80 miles an hour and reached Parkland Hospital within about four minutes.

Doctors worked desperately but in vain to save President Kennedy's life. At 1:20 P.M., Lyndon Johnson, waiting at the hospital, was told that John F. Kennedy was dead. Lyndon Baines Johnson was now President of the United States.

Governor Connally, though badly wounded, later made a full recovery.

The shots that killed the President had come from a sixth-floor window in the Texas School Book Depository Building, overlooking the motorcade route. A search of the building revealed a Mannlicher-Carcano 6.5 millimeter rifle near windows on the sixth floor. A palm print on the gun was identified as that of Lee Harvey Oswald, who worked in the building.

Oswald had fled after the shooting. Less than an hour later, in another part of the city, he shot and killed a Dallas policeman and attempted to shoot another before he was taken into custody.

Investigations by Secret Service and FBI agents and police left no doubt that Oswald was the assassin of the President. He never admitted it.

On Sunday morning, November 24, Dallas police prepared to transfer Oswald from police headquarters to the county jail. A crowd of newspaper reporters and policemen watched as Oswald was brought out. Suddenly one man, Jack Ruby, darted out from the crowd, pointed a revolver at the prisoner and fired one shot. Oswald was killed instantly. Ruby was arrested, and later died of cancer.

President Johnson appointed a special commission to make a thorough investigation of the assassination. The commission was headed by Earl Warren, Chief Justice of the United States, and its findings are set forth in the *Report of the President's Commission on the Assassination of President John F. Kennedy*—also known as *The Warren Report*.

Numerous books have been published about the report and the tragedy. There have been many rumors, theories and arguments about various aspects of the assassination, but the fact remains that the Secret Service performed its protective duty as efficiently as it could.

Quite a few people believe that the Secret Service can give orders to a President to help insure his personal safety, but this is not true. The Secret Service can only make suggestions. The President gives orders to the Secret Service. The Warren Commission was aware of the difficulties involved in security, and stated in its report:

> "The protection of the President of the United States is an immensely difficult and complex task. It is unlikely that measures can be devised to eliminate entirely the multitude of diverse dangers that may arise, particularly when the President is traveling in this country or abroad. The protective task is further complicated by the reluctance of Presidents to take security precautions which might interfere with the performance of their duties, or their desire to have frequent and easy access to the people."

President Kennedy was the fourth Chief Executive of the United States to be assassinated. The other three were Abraham Lincoln, James A. Garfield and William McKinley.

President Richard M. Nixon greets well-wishers on foreign soil. Secret Service men are there, as well, fulfilling their protective mission—on foot and in the car directly following the President.

Not until after the killing of President McKinley in 1901 was the Secret Service authorized to protect the President. For more than seventy years this duty has been performed capably and proudly by Secret Service agents prepared to give their own lives to save that of the President, if necessary.

But the Secret Service has other important work, too. In fact, it has been fighting crime effectively since it was organized in 1865, more than a hundred years ago.

Negotiable paper money in the United States has "come a long way" from the greenbacks of the early 1860's. Shown here, distinguishing features of the Andrew Jackson portrait on a counterfeit $20 bill are carefully scrutinized under a high-powered microscope.

Chapter 2

THE SECRET SERVICE BEGINS

In 1860, the paper money of the United States was not the same as it is now. Today, U.S. paper money is made by the Federal government, but in 1860 it was made only by banks.

Banks then were given special rights by their state governments to issue their own bank notes, or bills. Usually these could not be exchanged for gold or silver coins. They were simply supposed to circulate from person to person within each state, which meant that money issued by a bank in Massachusetts was not negotiable in New York or some other state.

Under this system, criminals discovered a way to operate a profitable racket. Two or three men would use political influence or bribery to get permission from state government officials to open a bank. They would put up a small building, maybe in an open field, and call it something like "The United Commercial Bank." Then they would hire a printer to print money bearing the bank's name, which they could use to buy all sorts of goods in their state. The goods had value, but the money was worthless.

There was another problem, too. Counterfeiters were producing imitations of genuine bank notes, and it was difficult for storekeepers and others to ascertain whether any bills were good or bad.

There were some gold and silver coins in circulation, and people began to hoard them because of the value of the ores of which they were made.

Because of this hoarding, all coins became scarce. As a replacement, some banks and even some private individuals issued a kind of paper money in small denominations. There were three-cent, five-cent, ten-cent and other pieces of this *fractional currency,* up to fifty cents. Because these were printed on pieces of paper smaller than that used for regular paper money, they were nicknamed "shinplasters," and people had to use them in place of metal coins.

This was the situation when the Civil War erupted in 1861. The Federal government—the Union—needed a strong currency, so the United States Treasury issued new $5, $10 and $20 bills, called "Treasury Demand Notes" because they were redeemable upon demand. This was the first paper money issued by the United States government. Because the backs of the bills were printed in green ink, people began to refer to them as "greenbacks."

During the next year, 1862, Congress authorized the government to issue another kind of paper money, called "United States Notes," in denominations of $1, $2, $5, $10, $20, $50, $100, $500 and $1,000.

Unlike the private bank notes, all of the government bills could be exchanged for gold and silver coins.

An early U.S. counterfeiter known as "Jim the Penman," Emanuel Ninger, passed more than $40,000 in hand-drawn notes for approximately fourteen years before being apprehended in March, 1896.

Now the counterfeiters had something new and better to copy, and they went at it in a big way. Most people were not yet familiar with the government bills, so even if a counterfeit was a poor imitation it could be passed without much difficulty. Bogus bills of every denomination began to show up in all parts of the country. In fact, it was estimated that about *one-third* of all paper money in circulation, both Federal and private bank notes, was counterfeit. That is, of every $100, about $33 was probably worthless.

People everywhere suffered losses as the victims of counterfeiters. Government officials were aware that if the public had no confidence in the new Federal paper money, the money would quickly lose in value. If that happened, the entire country could be in danger of a panic.

The Treasury Department offered rewards for the arrests and convictions of counterfeiters, but this produced few results. Then the department hired private detectives, but they were unable to find many of the hiding places where most of the bad money was produced.

The Secretary of the Treasury, Hugh McCulloch, visited the White House on April 14, 1865, and told President Abraham Lincoln that more effective methods would have to be found to fight the counterfeiters. The President asked if he had any suggestions.

"Yes," the Secretary said. "I think we should have a regular permanent force whose job it will be to put these counterfeiters out of business!"

Mr. Lincoln, tired and worn after four years of the war that had just ended, nodded slowly. "I think you have the right idea, Hugh," he said. "You work it out your own way."

Mr. McCulloch wrote later that these were the last words President Lincoln spoke to him. That night, the President was shot by John Wilkes Booth in Ford's Theater.

After inflicting the fatal shot to the head of President Abraham Lincoln, the assassin, John Wilkes Booth, leaped from the presidential box to the stage of Ford's Theater, catching his spur in the bunting and causing his ankle to snap in the fall. Despite the injury, he was nevertheless able to limp across the stage, flourishing a dagger and shouting, "Sic semper tyrannis!" ("Thus always to tyrants!") before effecting his escape in the confusion.

The President's death brought delays to some of the work of the Government, but within a few weeks Mr. McCulloch completed plans for his attack on the counterfeiters. To direct it, he chose William P. Wood, Warden of the Old Capitol Prison (see Chapter 17).

Mr. Wood knew a great deal about crooks and crime. He obtained all sorts of information from prisoners. Sometimes he went out himself and arrested men wanted for robbery or other offenses, including a few counterfeiters.

On July 5, 1865, Wood was sworn in as the first Chief of the new Treasury law-enforcement agency, the United States Secret Service.

During the Civil War there had been a "Secret Service" in the War Department, headed by Lafayette C. Baker, but it was a military organization similar to our modern military intelligence units. Allan Pinkerton, who later became famous as a private detective, worked for the War Department and was listed on its rolls as "Spy."

Chief Wood hired about thirty men as Secret Service "operatives." Some were private detectives who had worked on counterfeiting cases. Some were Wood's personal friends. A few were even former prisoners who had inside information about counterfeiters and their hideouts.

The mortally wounded President was carried across the street unconscious to a private house where members of the Cabinet later gathered with Mrs. Lincoln in a prayerful vigil. The President succumbed the following morning at 7:22 A.M.

Swindlers and confidence men have often deceived people by purporting to have an advanced technological invention which could duplicate genuine currency. The "green goods machine," shown here, suitably embellished with various dials and laboratory devices to create a semblance of scientific credibility, was just such a device.

The men began their work immediately. Some were sent into eleven cities where counterfeiters were most active, and worked undercover to infiltrate counterfeiting gangs. Week after week the Secret Service men, with the help of local police, raided one counterfeiting plant after another. Within its first year the Secret Service arrested more than two hundred engravers, printers, and passers of bogus bills, who were tried, convicted and sent to prison for long terms.

Whispers zipped through the underworld: "Watch out for your best friend. He may be a Secret Service man!"

By 1867 counterfeiting had been brought under control and people had gained confidence in the Government's paper money. More men had been added to the Secret Service, and new field offices were opened in various cities.

Although its original purpose was to fight counterfeiting, the Secret Service was the only general law-enforcement agency in the Federal Government. The Bureau of Customs was an older part of the Treasury Department, but it was concerned only with collecting customs duties on imported goods and preventing smuggling.

The Government needed investigators to combat other kinds of crime. Since the Secret Service was already in existence and was doing effective investigative work, it was natural that other departments of Government would call upon its agents to crack down on other kinds of lawbreakers.

Chapter 3

CRACKDOWN

On the cold, dark night of November 7, 1876, a squad of Secret Service agents and private detectives from the Pinkerton Detective Agency hid behind tombstones in a cemetery in Springfield, Illinois.

In the darkness they watched the dim outline of the tomb where the body of Abraham Lincoln rested. Secret Service Agent Patrick Tyrrell of Chicago had received information that two members of a counterfeiting gang, Jack Hughes and Terence Mullen, planned to steal Lincoln's body.

The reason? Hughes and Mullen wanted to get their partner, Ben Boyd, out of jail, where he was serving a ten-year sentence for counterfeiting. Boyd was an expert engraver, and his friends needed him to make plates for more bogus bills. Their idea was to steal Abraham Lincoln's body and then offer to return it if the Government would release Ben Boyd.

When word of the blackmail plot reached the Secret Service in Chicago, Agent Tyrrell reported it to his chief and also to Robert Lincoln, the late President's son. Robert Lincoln asked that Pinkerton detectives be permitted to work with the Secret Service, because Allan Pinkerton had been friendly with the Lincolns and had once acted as the President's bodyguard.

Hughes and Mullen arrived at the cemetery about nine o'clock. They sawed through a padlock to open the door of the tomb, and went inside. The agents and detectives began to close in slowly.

Suddenly a shot rang out in the blackness. One of the Pinkerton detectives had accidentally fired his percussion-cap pistol. It was so dark that the men couldn't see each other, and no one knew who had fired the shot, or why. They took cover behind tombstones, and some of the men began shooting at shadows. Within moments they identified each other by calling out, and the shooting stopped.

Agent Tyrrell rushed to the door of the tomb and pushed it wide open. "You in there!" he called. "Come out with your hands up! You're under arrest!"

There was no answer. Quickly Tyrrell stepped into the dark tomb. He stood still, listening. There was no sound. He struck a match and held it at arm's length. In the flickering light he saw that the tomb was empty except for the marble sarcophagus that held Lincoln's coffin.

The other men came in. They noticed that the lid of the sarcophagus had been removed and that the coffin had actually been slid out more than a foot. Obviously, Hughes and Mullen had been frightened off by the shot.

The next morning Tyrrell and his agents started a search for the fugitives. Hughes and Mullen were tracked down ten days after the attempted theft and were arrested by the Secret Service in Chicago on November 17. They were tried and convicted on May 31, 1877, and each was sentenced to a prison term.

This was only one of many unusual cases investigated by the Secret Service. Its agents were being called upon frequently to do all kinds of detective work for the Government.

In 1871, for example, the Attorney General had asked that the Secret Service investigate the activities of the Ku Klux Klan, which was terrorizing Negroes in North and South Carolina, Florida, Alabama and Georgia. Eight Secret Service agents were sent into those states and soon began to obtain results. Within three years the agents arrested and prosecuted more than a thousand Klan members and leaders, many of whom were sent to prison for ten years. The terrorist tactics came to a stop, at least for a long time.

Another kind of task was assigned to the Secret Service in 1898, when the United States was at war with Spain. The War Department asked the Secret Service to crack down on an elusive ring of Spanish spies.

The Chief of the Secret Service organized a special detail of Spanish-speaking agents to do this job. Working undercover, they learned the identities of spies in Washington, Florida, New York, Louisiana and California. Fitting the bits of information together like a jigsaw puzzle, the agents discovered that the spies operated under the direction of Señor Ramón Carranza. Carranza at one time had been a military attaché in the Spanish Legation in Washington, but had moved away. Agents located his secret headquarters in Montreal, Canada.

Ku Klux Klan members, wearing white robes and hoods, parade along Pennsylvania Avenue in Washington, D.C. The year: 1925.

The Secret Service men, assisted by Canadian police, exposed Carranza's spy plots, and the Canadian Government ordered him to leave the country.

There were many other Secret Service crackdowns in the early days. Agents in New York, for instance, smashed widespread extortion rackets of the Mafia and arrested members of Mafia "families" who were making counterfeit money.

In the 1900's, agents also broke up the crooked Louisiana Lottery, a gambling venture that started operating in 1862 and later obtained a license from the state of Louisiana. After a scandal revealed that the lottery was "fixed," the operators moved to Honduras in Central America. Most of their lottery tickets were sold in the United States. In the drawings, the big prizes went to the crooked lottery operators, while the legitimate participants received few prizes, if any.

Secret Service agents discovered that the lottery tickets were being printed in the United States. After months of investigation, the agents located the print shop, seized thousands of tickets, and arrested the operators. They indicted twenty-four men, including five millionaires, and the crooked lottery was finally put out of business.

In 1901 a new and vital responsibility fell on Secret Service shoulders. President William McKinley was assassinated, and Congress later directed that succeeding Presidents should be protected by the Secret Service (see Chapter 12).

In 1907 President Theodore Roosevelt sent Secret Service agents to the Western frontier to investigate suspected frauds involving Government-owned land. Millions of acres were open to homesteaders who would build homes and raise farm crops, helping to settle and tame what was still the wild, wild West. But there were wealthy cattle ranchers who wanted the land—not only as grazing grounds for their herds, but also to dig coal and cut timber wherever these could be found.

The cattle barons paid war veterans small sums to file homestead claims. When the claims were granted, the veterans moved away and the cattlemen took over.

In making their investigations, the Secret Service agents met with obstacles everywhere. One agent was murdered (see Chapter 11). Despite attempts to interfere with the investigation, the agents unearthed evidence showing that millions of acres of homestead land had been obtained by fraud. Even more important, the agents brought to court two United States Senators and a Congressman who were allegedly involved in the land thefts.

This one courageous act caused tremendous harm to the Secret Service. The two Senators and the Congessman were not convicted, but other members of Congress angrily declared that the Secret Service should no longer do any work that was not directly connected with the Treasury Department—no more spy cases, no more investigations of the Ku Klux Klan or the Mafia, no more crackdowns on any crooked activities except counterfeiting of the currency and forgery of Government checks and bonds.

President Theodore Roosevelt tried in vain to reason with the Congress, pointing out that the Secret Service was doing a very effective law-enforcement job. The lawmakers, he said, had no reason to be upset unless they had guilty consciences. But Congress restricted the Secret Service duties to Treasury matters.

As a result, on July 1, 1908, President Roosevelt transferred eight Secret Service agents to the Department of Justice. They started what is now the Federal Bureau of Investigation (FBI).

In 1918 World War I was raging in Europe, and the United States was soon to be drawn into it. But while this country was still neutral, Germany organized a sabotage network here to work against France, England and the United States. President Woodrow Wilson ordered that the Congressional restriction on the Secret Service be lifted temporarily so the Secret Service could try to break up the German sabotage plot.

Secret Service agents soon identified Dr. Heinrich Albert as the German Government official who had been sent to New York to direct the saboteurs. One Secret Service agent, the late Frank Burke, succeeded in stealing a mysterious briefcase that rarely left Dr. Albert's hands. The case contained papers revealing the entire scheme. Albert's plans included the purchase of certain U.S. newspapers in which German propaganda would be printed; the purchase of ammunition factories where shells ordered by the Allies would never be shipped or would be made defective; and control of cotton and other markets essential to the French and English war effort.

The incriminating papers created a national sensation when they were front-paged in the New York *World,* and as a result Dr. Albert and his associates in the German diplomatic corps were sent back to Germany.

One of the Germans later wrote: "The loss of the Albert papers was as disastrous as the loss of the Marne."

After this achievement, the Governmental lid was again clamped down upon the Secret Service until the 1920's. Then, once again, the Secret Service was chosen by President Calvin Coolidge to investigate the Teapot Dome oil scandals.

Teapot Dome was the name of an area of public land in Wyoming where a few private companies had been permitted to drill for oil. In 1921, during the administration of President Warren G. Harding, a plot was hatched by greedy men to make millions of dollars from the Government's oil reserves. Two members of the President's Cabinet were involved.

One was Albert B. Fall of New Mexico, Secretary of the Interior. The other was Harry M. Daugherty, Attorney General of the United States. They conspired with officers of big oil companies to lease the whole Teapot Dome oil reserve to the "Mammoth Oil Company" without the knowledge of Congress. The entire deal had been completed as quietly as possible and was highly complicated because of the number of people and companies that were involved.

As a result of the Secret Service investigation, which was conducted without fanfare, Albert Fall was convicted and sent to prison. Others were fined or fled the country to escape prosecution.

After this successful investigation, the restrictions were once again imposed upon the Secret Service, and its agents went back to tracking counterfeiters and forgers.

This is still one of the major law-enforcement tasks of the Service, and because of new techniques and developments in printing and copying processes, more counterfeit money is being produced today than ever.

All equipment and supplies used in the manufacture of counterfeit currency are subject to seizure by the Federal Government. Above, an offset press with impressions of counterfeit bills still visible on its rollers, as found by Secret Service agents.

Chapter 4

THE BOGUS BILL BUSINESS

Some time ago a Hungarian-refugee family arrived in the United States carrying their life's savings of about eleven hundred dollars. When they tried to deposit the money in a New York bank they were told that it was all counterfeit. They had bought the bills at a higher-than-official rate of exchange in the European black market and had been completely cheated. Now they didn't have a dime.

Similar tragedies have struck other refugees who were not familiar with the designs of United States paper money. Sadly enough, few Americans pay any attention to these designs, either, so they are as naive as the foreigner and are easy marks for passers of counterfeit bills.

Counterfeiting is the only *specific* crime that the Constitution of the United States empowers Congress to punish (Article I, Section 8). Counterfeiting is also one of the most difficult crimes to fight, because every move of the counterfeiter is aimed at concealment. He may set up his press and equipment in some dingy attic or cellar, or in an isolated farmhouse, or even in a printing shop that does legitimate business. The counterfeiter who does his fraudulent work after regular hours in a printing shop is often as inconspicuous as a tombstone in a cemetery.

While many counterfeiters are lone wolves, acting as both manufacturers and passers, others set up organizations that are run in businesslike fashion. For example, one or two men with (real) money and not much skill may finance the operation. They hire a photographer and a printer, or they may be fortunate enough to get one craftsman who can qualify as both.

The manufacturer sells the output of the plant—the bogus bills—to one or more trusted "distributors," or wholesalers. The yield of an active plant might consist of counterfeit bills representing as much as a million dollars or even more.

The distributor may buy the counterfeits for as little as five or six cents on the dollar. In other words, one hundred dollars in bogus bills would cost him five or six dollars in genuine money, depending upon the quantity he buys.

He now offers the product to salesmen, or retailers, for perhaps ten or twelve cents on the dollar ($10 or $12 per $100), sometimes more.

The salesmen increase the price as they see fit, because their customers are the last in line—the passers. Passers may pay anywhere from fifteen to thirty-five or forty cents on the dollar for the "queer," according to the amount bought. Ironically, they also take the biggest chances of being caught, and if they are arrested they usually have no knowledge of the identity of the manufacturer, or even of the distributors.

To minimize the risk of capture, passers often operate in devious ways. One way is to approach a child on the street and pay him a dime or quarter to go to a grocery store to buy a loaf of bread with a counterfeit bill. The passer loiters near the store as the youngster makes the purchase. If the grocer questions the bill and the child, or makes a telephone call, the passer is usually off and running. But if the purchase goes through, he collects his change from the boy or girl and will either give away the bread or throw it into the nearest trash can and look for his next victim.

Not infrequently, teen-agers are drawn into the racket in this way. The teen-ager makes the first purchase in good faith, and if it succeeds he is paid perhaps a dollar or two by the passer, who asks, "How'd you like to make some more easy money, kid?" Once the "kid" *deliberately* passes another counterfeit, knowing it to be bad, he's on the same criminal footing as the Fagin who trapped him.

One case in upper New York State was disastrous for two teen-age boys, Tony, 18, and Frank, 19. They bought a supply of counterfeit bills which they intended to pass on merchants in a small town. They drove to the outskirts of the town, arriving about three o'clock in the morning, and decided to park their car and wait until the stores opened.

The entire supply of the counterfeit money was in Frank's pocket. Tony suggested that they divide it equally. Frank refused and got out of the car. Tony followed. In the darkness they paced up and down the side of the road, cursing each other. Tony suddenly yanked out a revolver and shot Frank to death.

He dragged the body into a nearby quarry, took all the counterfeits from Frank's pockets, along with Frank's watch and ring, then drove into town. When the stores opened, Tony started on a spending spree. He passed two of the bills without difficulty. When he tried to pass the third in a drugstore, the druggist refused to accept it. Tony walked out with the bill, but the druggist followed him until he saw a policeman. The druggist told the officer about Tony and the counterfeit money. The policeman arrested Tony, found the other bills in his pockets, and the gun he had used to kill Frank. But as yet they didn't know about Frank's murder.

The police notified the Secret Service, and agents questioned Tony. He refused to say where he had obtained the counterfeits. Agents examined his revolver and established that it had been fired very recently. Tony claimed he had shot at a bird, but the next day a farmer discovered Frank's body in the quarry, and agents and police were able to prove that the fatal bullet had come from Tony's gun.

Tony confessed to the murder and was sentenced to life imprisonment.

Counterfeiting is not a small-time minor crime. It is aimed at the pocketbook of the average citizen, so it is a crime against the people. It has also been used successfully by foreign governments as a powerful weapon of war. For example, the value of the Continental currency of the American Revolution was reduced to zero when the British dumped tons of counterfeits into circulation—and the expression, "not worth a Continental," is still in use today.

This act may have set the pattern for the ruin of the assignat currency issued by the French Revolutionary Government in 1789. Enemies of the revolution counterfeited the new French money so extensively that by 1796 there were more than fifteen *billion* counterfeit francs in circulation. Result: the assignat became worthless and was repudiated by the French Government.

In 1812 Napoleon Bonaparte, Emperor of France, set up an elaborate counterfeiting plant in the heart of Paris and ordered the manufacture of counterfeit money which he then used to buy guns and military supplies for his invasion of Russia.

Closer to our own time was the wholesale counterfeiting of British and other foreign currencies sponsored by Adolf Hitler, who combed his concentration camps to find expert engravers, printers and other craftsmen held as prisoners. They were assembled in a special compound at one of the death camps and ordered to make counterfeit passports, identification cards and other documents for the use of Nazi spies—but their primary task became the production of counterfeit English money. Much of it was so well made that it actually defied detection by British banks. The prisoners were just beginning to make counterfeit United

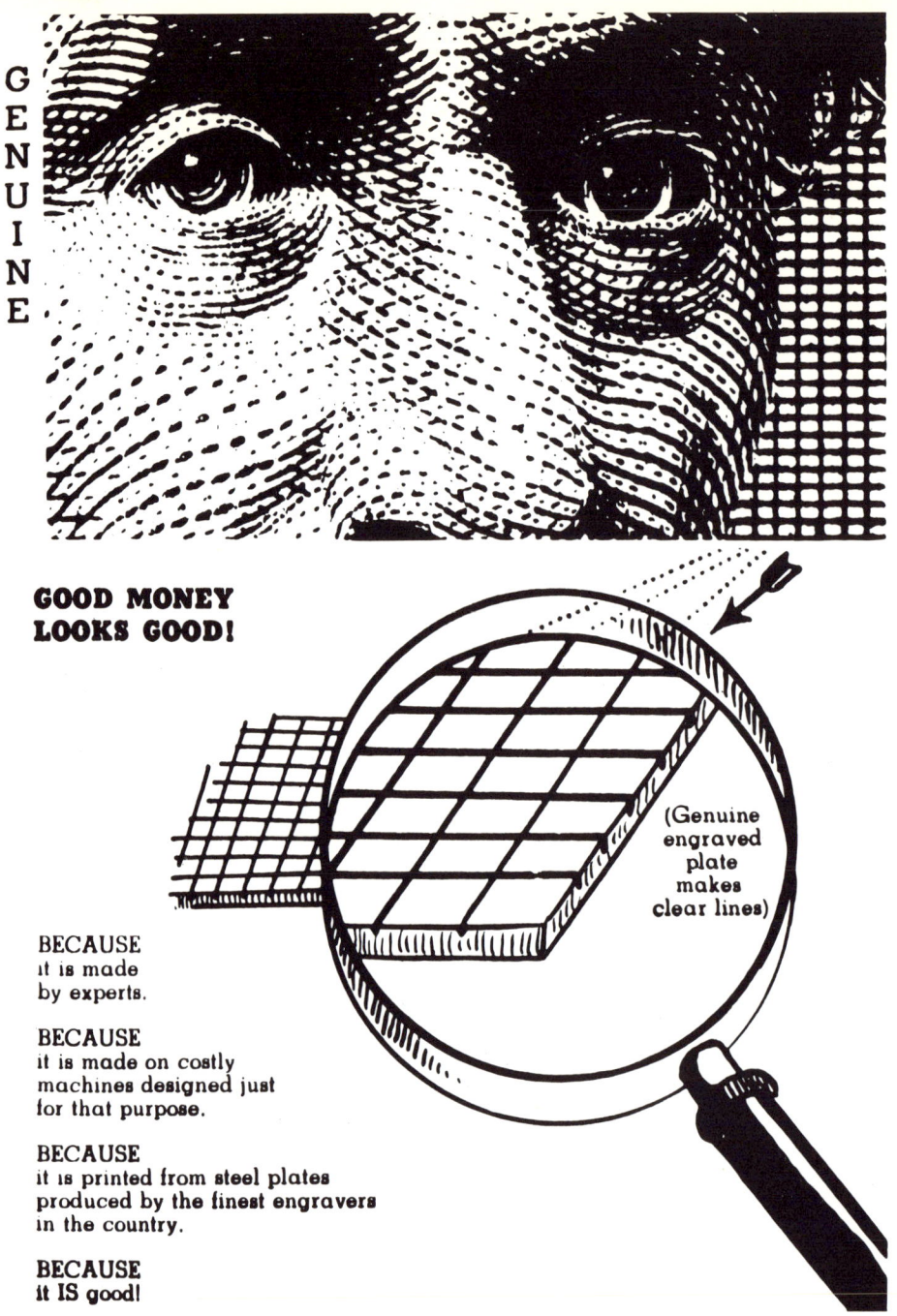

GOOD MONEY LOOKS GOOD!

BECAUSE it is made by experts.

BECAUSE it is made on costly machines designed just for that purpose.

BECAUSE it is printed from steel plates produced by the finest engravers in the country.

BECAUSE it IS good!

States currency when the Allied advance brought their operations to a halt.

One lesson to be learned from history is that runaway large-scale counterfeiting can ruin a nation's economy. Uncontrolled, it could cause disastrous inflation, devaluation of the American dollar, and financial chaos.

Years ago a skilled counterfeiter had to be a good engraver and printer. Today, modern methods of photography and printing make counterfeiting relatively easy. They also make more difficult the work of

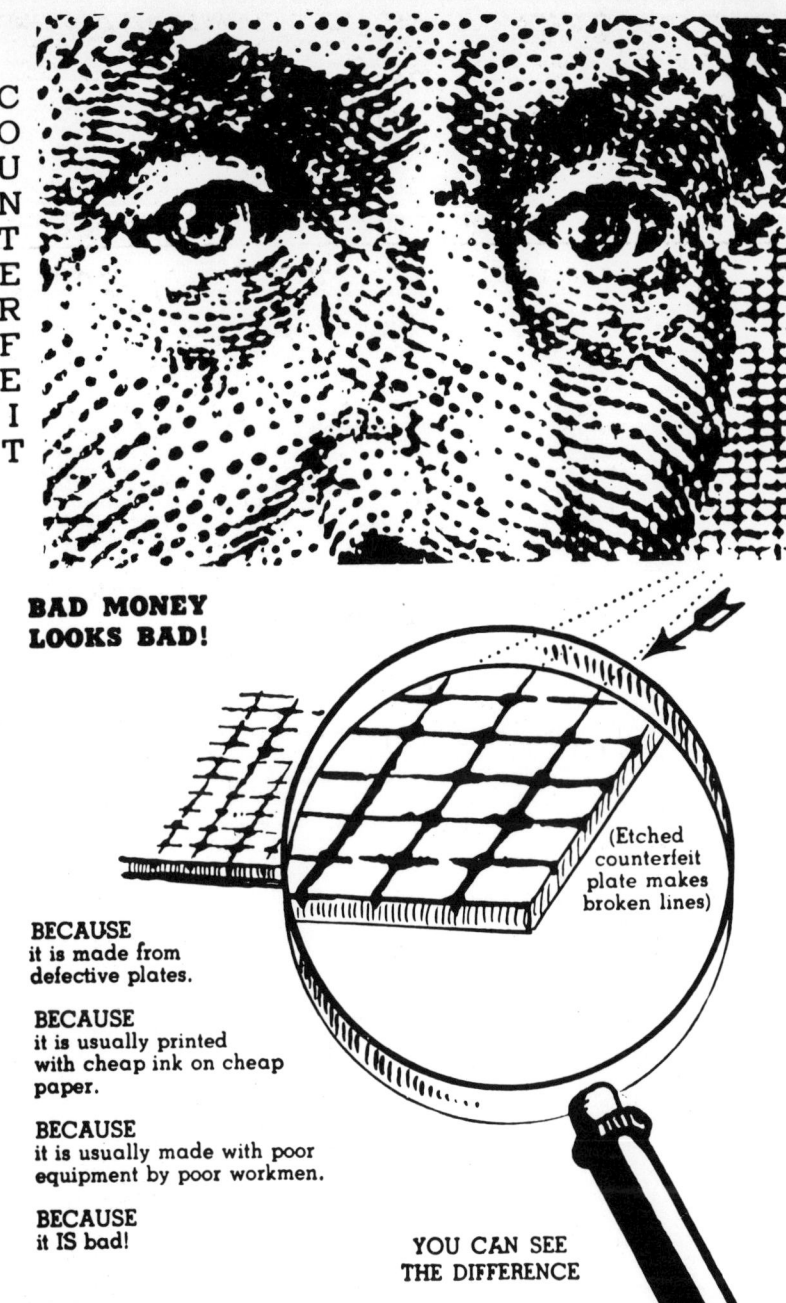

Magnification reveals the well-defined lines of a genuine U.S. bill (opposite page) and the fuzzy, imperfect lines of a counterfeit (this page).

the Secret Service in fighting this type of crime, yet its agents continue to do their jobs so effectively that none of us ever stops to consider that the money in our pockets might be homemade.

In a typical year the Secret Service arrested some 1,400 people for violating the counterfeiting laws, and captured more than fifteen million dollars in bogus money before it could get into circulation.

Many of these and other cases were developed through the efficient and sometimes dangerous work of important members of the Secret Service team—the undercover agents.

Chapter 5

UNDERCOVER AGENT

An undercover agent pretends to be a criminal in order to observe the unlawful acts of real criminals and to get evidence that will lead to their arrest and conviction.

Because an undercover agent must pose as something he isn't, he must be a first-class actor. Unlike the stage actor, however, the undercover agent plays "for keeps," and if he fails to be convincing in his role he might wind up dead.

In one case, an informant reported to the Secret Service in New York City that he knew a man who had a supply of counterfeit money. The informant agreed to introduce an undercover agent to the suspect, nicknamed "Cowboy." They met in the waiting room of a bus terminal.

Cowboy was cautious at first, asking questions about the agent's background. How many times had he been arrested? What for? Any convictions? Who were his friends or contacts in the underworld?

The groundwork had been carefully laid for the undercover agent's answers to such questions, but after he answered some of them he pretended to become impatient.

"Listen, friend," he said, "you want to do business or not? If you don't, just say so now, and I'll find another connection."

"Okay, okay," Cowboy said. "Don't get so uptight. I gotta protect myself and my brother Willie. You understand?"

"Your brother? What's he got to do with it?"

"He's in it with me. We're partners."

"So? Do we have a deal or not?"

"How much stuff you want?" Cowboy asked.

"Depends on the price," the agent said. "If it's too high, forget it."

"Twenty bucks a hundred. And it's all top stuff."

"That's what you say. How do I know?"

Cowboy took a $10, a $20 and a $100 bill from his jacket pocket and handed them to the agent. "Take these over to the telephone booth and look for yourself," he said, glancing at some of the people in the terminal.

The agent went to the booth and examined the bills. They were only of fair quality. He returned to the bench. "You call this top stuff? You'd better have your eyes examined. Some kid must've made 'em." He handed the bills back to Cowboy, who pocketed them.

"You want 'em or not?" Cowboy asked.

"Not at twenty a hundred. They're not worth it."

"How much, then?"

Below, composite portraits of Abraham Lincoln and Alexander Hamilton, as found on both counterfeit and genuine $5 and $10 bills. The definition apparent on the right-hand side of each portrait is in marked contrast to the counterfeit (left-hand) sides.

The agent shrugged. "Oh, about ten, maybe."

"Ten! You're outa your mind. Forget it." Cowboy started to get up. The agent put a hand on his arm.

"Okay, okay. Twelve."

"Fifteen."

"I said twelve. That's it. And remember—I want a big bundle."

"All right, twelve—but only if you'll take a hundred grand."

"A hundred grand?" The agent paused. "Well, I was thinking about fifty grand—but okay. It's a deal. What about delivery?"

"We'll deliver in Philly tomorrow night. Meet my brother and me and have your dough ready. And come alone." Cowboy mentioned the name of a Philadelphia hotel and a room number.

The following day, based on the undercover agent's report, the Secret Service tried to rent the adjoining room in the hotel, but it was not available, so arrangements were made to have other agents stationed in the room across the hall. It was agreed that after the undercover agent met Cowboy and his brother, making sure that they had the counterfeit money, the agent would say that he had to leave to get the cash. If he stepped into the corridor, this would be a signal to the agents across the hall to make the arrests.

At the appointed time the undercover agent met Cowboy and his brother Willie in the hotel room. Willie was a six-footer with long, stringy brown hair, a ragged mustache, and wore blue jeans, a bright pink shirt with a dark stain near the collar, and a green Apache tie.

A suitcase was on the bed, and after shaking hands with the agent, Willie opened the case, which was filled with counterfeit bills and a submachine gun. Willie picked up the gun and pointed it at the agent.

"Hey, watch that thing!" the agent exclaimed. "What's the idea?"

"Ain't you never heard about hijacking?" Cowboy said, grinning. "We just don't want you to leave with the stuff before we finish our deal."

"You just tell Willie to be careful, that's all."

The agent took some of the bills from the suitcase and examined them.

"You don't have to count it," Cowboy said. "We threw in a few extra pieces, just in case some ain't as good as others."

"Okay. I trust you, because we may want to make other deals later." The agent added, "I'll be back in a few minutes," and started for the door.

"Hold it!" Willie said. He held the gun inches from the agent's chest. "Where you goin', pal?"

The agent grinned. "To get the dough, of course." He glanced at Cowboy. "Haven't you heard of hijacking, Cowboy? You don't think I'd have twelve grand in real cash on me, do you? I left it downstairs in the hotel safe."

The brothers looked at each other. "Okay, then," Cowboy said. "I'll go down with you. Willie will stay here with the stuff."

The agent opened the door and stepped into the hall, followed by Cowboy, as Willie watched. Immediately, three agents stepped out of the room across the hall. Two seized Cowboy and the agent. The third rushed toward Willie.

Willie slammed the door. Quickly he pushed the bed against it. Agents heard the sound of breaking glass, but they were on the third floor and knew Willie couldn't jump to safety. One agent sped to the lobby and got from the manager a key to the adjoining room and a key to the door connecting both rooms. Occupants of the adjoining room were out.

The agents hauled Cowboy with them out of the hall and into the adjoining room. With guns drawn they unlocked the connecting door and pushed it open. One leaped into the room. Willie stood in the center of the floor, pointing the machine gun at the agent. Willie kept pulling the trigger, his face contorted with rage and frustration as the gun failed to fire. Within seconds the agents were upon him and wrested the weapon from his big hands.

With both prisoners under control, the agents examined the submachine gun—and laughed! They actually laughed. The gun hadn't fired because Willie had put the bullets into it *backwards!* Perhaps it was funny, in a way—but if it hadn't been for Willie's stupidity, the episode might have turned into a shootout with a tragic ending for the agents and for Cowboy and Willie as well.

Seeking leniency, the brothers led agents to their counterfeiting plant. Both were convicted and sentenced to long terms in a Federal penitentiary.

The undercover agent who infiltrates a criminal gang may play such a convincing part that when it becomes necessary for him to reveal his identity, the gang refuses to believe him. In one such case an undercover agent was allowed to visit a counterfeiting plant in a ghetto apartment, just before the plant was to be moved to a new secret location. Other agents could not keep him under surveillance without being detected.

Once inside the plant, the agent decided to arrest the counterfeiters who had accepted him for weeks as one of their number. For obvious reasons he was not carrying his Secret Service credentials, and when he suddenly held the members of the gang at gunpoint and announced that he was a Secret Service agent, they jeered.

"You lousy hijacker!" one said.

"You'll never get away with it," another added.

The head of the gang nodded slowly. "Go ahead," he said. "Take the stuff. But you better hide and hide good, because we'll come lookin' for you."

An agent compares an old counterfeit bill with a more recent one. Details of workmanship often offer clues to the possible identification of a known counterfeiter who has returned to his "trade."

Not until the agent called his associates, who confirmed the fact that he was a Secret Service man, did the gang members believe it.

The undercover agent, whether he's in the Secret Service, the FBI, the State Police, the local police department, or in some other branch of law enforcement, is truly the unsung hero of the fight against crime. Usually he tries to avoid testifying in open court in order to keep his identity a secret. To be successful in his purpose he has to associate with thieves, drug pushers and addicts, killers, counterfeiters, forgers and other unsavory denizens of the underworld. He faces some element of danger in almost every assignment, yet he does so with the full realization of the possible consequences—and all because he is completely dedicated to serving the cause of law, order and justice.

Chapter 6

THE COINERS

One day the principal of a high school in a New York City suburb reported that he had found a number of counterfeit quarters in candy vending machines at the school. A Secret Service agent was sent to investigate.

The agent examined the coins. They were so poorly made that they couldn't fool anybody. That was undoubtedly the reason they were used in machines and not passed in stores.

There were no clues to show who had used the coins, but the agent suspected that they had been made by one of the students.

"That may be," the principal said, "but which one?"

"I have an idea," the agent said. "Can you call a general assembly in the auditorium?"

The principal called the assembly. When all the boys and girls were present, he introduced the Secret Service agent.

"I'm here on a very serious mission," the agent told the students. "A number of counterfeit coins have been used in the vending machines in this school. My investigation indicates that these coins were made by a student." He paused and looked at all the faces. "However, before I make an arrest, I want you all to realize that counterfeiting is a very serious crime. In fact, the one who made and used these bad quarters, if convicted, could be sent to prison for ten years. Ten years! But if he willingly gives himself up now, he—"

Suddenly several boys and girls stood up. There was a murmur of voices, then one boy turned toward the stage and shouted, "He's fainted! Frankie's fainted!"

Frankie, a tall thin boy with blond hair, was taken to the principal's office and treated by the school nurse. After he felt better, the Secret Service man said to him, "How many coins did you make, Frankie?"

The boy looked down at the floor. "I only made twenty," he answered. "Five dollars' worth."

"Did anyone help you?"

"No." He looked up. "I'm sorry. I didn't realize how serious it was."

Frankie was brought into court as a juvenile offender. He was placed on probation for a year.

This was an unusual case because it involved only one 15-year-old boy and a handful of counterfeit quarters. In other cases the Secret Service has arrested many adults for making counterfeit pennies, nickels, dimes, quarters, half-dollars and silver dollars.

The gains to be made from passing bogus coins are small, and if a passer gets caught he may spend years in prison. A more profitable crime involves changing the appearance of ordinary coins to make them look like expensive rare coins. These would be of numismatic value. (Numismatics relates to the study of coins, medals and paper money.)

In Milwaukee, Wisconsin, a coin collector we'll call Howard bought a dime for $100 from a man named Jimmy. The dime bore the date 1916 and would ordinarily be worth about $1.40 to a collector. But this particular coin had the capital letter "D" after the date, indicating that the coin was made at the Denver Mint. Since very few 1916-D dimes are in existence, one in very fine condition is worth as much as $220 to numismatists. Even a one-cent coin bearing the date 1909-S (for San Francisco), together with the initials "VDB" (for Victor D. Brenner, the coin designer), could be worth $100 or more if it were genuine.

Howard, the coin collector, later thought the capital "D" on the 1916 dime looked a bit crooked. He brought the dime to the Secret Service, where a laboratory examination showed that the "D" had been added to an ordinary 1916 coin.

An undercover agent arranged for Howard to introduce him to Jimmy, the man who had sold Howard the dime. The agent posed as a possible buyer of other coins and became friendly with Jimmy. At a table in a small restaurant they talked about prices for "rare" pennies and dimes.

"Listen, pal," the agent said, "don't kid me any longer. Those coins have to be phony to sell at such low prices. If you can guarantee that they're good jobs and if you want to do business, I've got connections that can handle a good piece of the action." He took a roll of bills from his pocket and showed it to Jimmy, then put it back.

Jimmy waved one hand back and forth. "No, no, Mac," he said, "you've got it all wrong. The coins ain't phony—honest."

The agent shrugged his shoulders and stood up. "Okay, Jimmy," he said. "I guess I can do business somewhere else. No hard feelings." He offered to shake hands.

"Wait a second, Mac," Jimmy said. "Sit down for a minute."

The agent sat down. In a low voice Jimmy said, "Okay, we can do business. But not here. I have to talk to the boss."

"Who's the boss?"

"Never mind. He's got the stuff and he does the work on the coins."

"I want to talk to him."

"What about?"

"About wholesale prices. And I want his personal guarantee that the coins will stand up under testing by collectors."

"He won't talk to strangers," Jimmy said.

"Okay, so that's that. I'll see you around." The agent stood up again and started for the door.

"Hold it!" Jimmy said. "I'll ask him. I'll call you tonight."

The agent gave Jimmy his home telephone number. That night he received a call from Jimmy saying that the boss would meet them the next evening at midnight.

At the appointed time the undercover agent arrived at the small hotel where the boss lived. Other agents took up positions in an adjoining room, from which they could overhear conversations.

Jimmy introduced the agent to the short, fat boss, called Maxie. Maxie showed the agent five pennies and ten dimes bearing mint marks with the dates. "You can peddle this for about two grand," he said.

"What's your price?" the agent asked.

"Ordinarily a thousand, but for you a special. Nine hundred sixty-five. And you get your dough back if they aren't okay."

The agent objected. They dickered. The agent examined the coins carefully, finally paid Maxie $900 and took the coins. Then the agents from the next room came in and arrested Jimmy and Maxie.

"Hey," Jimmy said. "You know what? I was just going to call you guys."

A search of the room revealed about three hundred dollars in pennies and dimes to which Maxie had added mint marks and initials. If they had been genuine rare coins, they would have been worth as much as $40,000 to collectors.

Maxie and Jimmy both pleaded guilty and were fined and sentenced to prison terms.

If the altered coins had been sold to collectors, many or all of the coins might still be treasured as genuine, since the alterations were expertly done. This is not always the case with counterfeit coins and paper money, however, and there are ways in which the average person can tell the difference between good and bad coins and bills.

Genuine U.S. coins having a value greater than (and including) a dime have clearly defined and evenly spaced ridges—known as the reeding—along the outer edge. The reeding on counterfeit coins is usually uneven, crooked, and often missing.

Chapter 7

BAD MONEY LOOKS BAD

One summer afternoon a small boy walked into a grocery store near Philadelphia to buy a loaf of bread. He handed the grocer a quarter. The grocer stared at the coin, then dropped it on the counter. It fell with a dull thud.

"This quarter isn't any good," the clerk said.

"It must be good," the boy answered. "My daddy just cooked it."

The storekeeper telephoned the Secret Service. Soon agents arrested the boy's father for making counterfeit coins from melted metal.

Dropping a bad coin on a hard surface is sometimes the only test needed to detect it. But some counterfeiters have made coins that have a ring almost as clear as that of genuine coins. In such cases you must use your eyes rather than your ears to tell the good from the bad.

What should you look for? First, look at those little ridges around the outer rim of dimes, quarters, half-dollars and silver dollars. These are called the "reeding." This feature is one that's hard for most coin counterfeiters to imitate perfectly. On a genuine coin these ridges are straight and evenly spaced. On the average counterfeit there will be one small section of the reeding where a few ridges are crooked or even missing. This is a defect in the method of making the coins, and sometimes the counterfeiter tries to fill in the gap by using a file to make crude ridges.

You should also inspect the lettering on the coin, and the rest of the design. Now and then these features have been retouched by hand and are obviously defective or not quite the same as those on genuine coins.

Many counterfeit coins feel greasy to the touch. If you rub one between your thumb and forefinger, the slippery feeling is often very noticeable.

Occasionally there are counterfeit coins so well made that only an expert can detect them. If you should happen to receive one of these in change, the chances are that it will pass from hand to hand until it reaches a bank. Bank tellers are generally adept at discovering bad coins or bills, which are then surrendered to the Secret Service.

Detecting counterfeit bills may be fairly easy or very difficult, depending upon their quality.

Do you happen to know any identical twins? Sometimes people can't tell which is which when they see only one twin. But when the twins are together there are usually some physical differences that make it easy to identify one from the other. It's much the same with genuine and counterfeit bills.

If you think a bill might be counterfeit, one of the first things to do is to compare it with one of the same kind that you *know* is genuine. When the two are placed side by side—like the twins—perhaps you will see differences in the color, or notice that the serial numbers on one are crooked or imperfect.

A reproduction of the Treasury seal appears on every bill. It looks like a circular saw because it's surrounded by sawteeth. On a genuine bill these teeth are sharp and clear. On most counterfeits some of the points may be broken or rounded off.

The borders of United States paper money are made up of a spider-webby network of fine lines called "lathework." On a genuine bill these lines are clear and unbroken. On most counterfeits many of the lines may be incomplete or missing in places.

Every bill also has the portrait of a famous American in an oval on its face. If you look closely, you'll see that the background of the portrait is made up of very fine crosshatch lines that form tiny squares, like those of a window screen. On a genuine bill these squares are readily seen. But on most counterfeits many of the squares become filled with ink because the lines are so close together that the counterfeiter has difficulty keeping the spaces between them clean.

COUNTERFEIT GENUINE

Every U.S. bill bears a reproduction of the Treasury seal. Again, the clearly defined features (see above) help distinguish a genuine bill from a counterfeit.

The same thing also applies to the lines that make up the features of the faces in the portraits. Many of these lines are really dots and dashes, and the counterfeiter often has trouble getting them all in. If some are left out, they create white spots on the face in places where there shouldn't be white spots.

Look at the eyes in the portrait. On the genuine bill the eyes are clear and lifelike. On many counterfeits they are dull or blurred.

43

Engraved portraits of notable Americans appear on the various denominations of U.S. paper currency. These likenesses may be found on $1, $5, $10, $20, $50, and $100 bills.

Did you know that you can tell the denomination of a bill by its portrait? For example:

George Washington is only on $1 bills.
Thomas Jefferson is only on $2 bills.
Abraham Lincoln is only on $5 bills.
Alexander Hamilton is only on $10 bills.
Andrew Jackson is only on $20 bills.
Ulysses S. Grant is only on $50 bills.
Benjamin Franklin is only on $100 bills.
William McKinley is only on $500 bills.
Grover Cleveland is only on $1,000 bills.
James Madison is only on $5,000 bills.
Salmon P. Chase is only on $10,000 bills.

Sometimes criminals try to change a real $5 bill to make it look like a $20 bill. If you ever see a $20 bill with Abraham Lincoln's picture, you'll know that it can't be a genuine $20 bill.

If you should ever receive a counterfeit coin or bill, DON'T try to spend it. Turn it in at the nearest office of the Secret Service, or to your local police department, and tell where and how you got it.

If you want more information about detecting counterfeit money, you can buy a Secret Service booklet entitled *Know Your Money* from the Superintendent of Documents, Government Printing Office, Washington, D.C. 20402. It costs 25 cents.

The booklet also carries some interesting information about redeeming paper money that has been torn, burned or mutilated in some other way. There are unscrupulous people who try to cheat the Treasury by such mutilation.

A high-speed currency printing press in use at the Bureau of Engraving and Printing.

Chapter 8

LIES FOR LOOT

If you should happen to find the torn half of a genuine $5 or $10 bill, you could turn it in to the Treasury Department and get half of its original value—that is, $2.50 or $5.00.

If you could furnish good proof that the missing half had been totally destroyed, you could get the *full* value of the bill—$5, or $10, or whatever the denomination was.

Redemption of mutilated currency is governed by Treasury Department regulations. They provide that if a person has a piece of a genuine bill that is more than two-fifths but less than three-fifths of the whole bill, he may be paid one-half of the value of the bill.

If his fragment is as large as three-fifths or more of the whole bill, the Treasury will pay him full face value.

If the piece is *less* than two-fifths of the whole bill, it is worthless— *unless* the holder can furnish satisfactory proof that the missing portion has been completely destroyed. If the Treasury accepts such proof, the holder will receive the full face value of the bill.

Knowing this, many people over the years have tried to cheat the Treasury by making false claims for mutilated money.

As one example, a bank in Albany, New York, sent the Treasury three halves of $100 bills. The Treasury paid the bank $50 for each half.

About six weeks later the Treasury received three halves of $100 bills, the edges of which had been charred by fire. They came from a man we'll call Spence, living in New York City. The serial numbers on

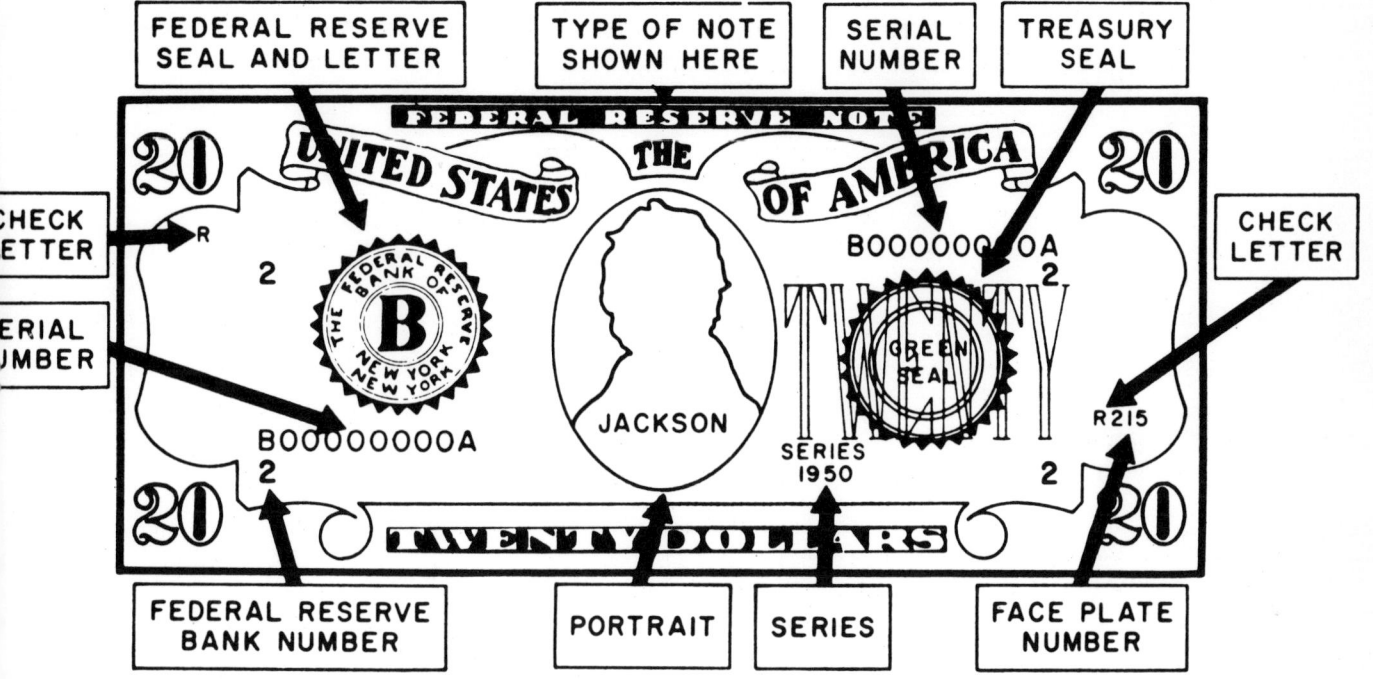

Various basic design features of a $20 Federal Reserve Note are disclosed here.

these three halves were the same as those on the three pieces sent in by the Albany bank. In other words, these were the missing parts of the unburned Albany fragments.

Spence sent the Treasury an affidavit swearing that he had kept the three whole $100 bills in an envelope in a dresser drawer in his home. He claimed that his five-year-old nephew had found the envelope and burned it while playing with matches, destroying half of each bill. Spence asked the Treasury to pay him three hundred dollars—but of course he did not know that the Treasury had already redeemed the three other halves of the same bills.

The Redemption Division of the Treasury Department sent the facts and the charred pieces to the Secret Service for investigation.

A Secret Service agent questioned Spence and showed him the unburned halves of the three bills received from the Albany bank.

"How do you explain that?" the agent asked.

"Oh, that. Yes. Well, you see, at one time I thought I had left those bills in the glove compartment of my car. The car was stolen and wrecked. Yes, that must be what happened. I left them in the glove compartment."

"How could that be, when your affidavit says that the halves of the notes were found in your dresser drawer?"

"Oh," Spence said, "the police who investigated the car accident gave me some papers they found in the car. I must have taken the envelope out of the drawer and put it in my car with other papers. And the papers must have included the burned bills."

The agent checked with police and learned that the glove compartment of Spence's car contained only three unimportant papers, which the police were still holding. Also, he learned that when the car was wrecked, it had not caught fire.

Now the investigation shifted to Albany. Through information obtained at the bank, agents were led to a local tavern. There they learned that two nationally known male entertainers had visited the tavern in company with a man who had a pocketful of money. During the evening this man became friendly with a girl who worked in the place. He took out three $100 bills, tore them in half, and gave three halves to the woman. He said she could get the other pieces by coming to his hotel room. She refused, but she kept the torn money.

Later, the girl gave the torn bills to the bartender in the tavern. He showed them to a friend named Phil, who thought they could be redeemed. Phil took them to the Albany bank and eventually received $150, which he had agreed to split with the bartender, but never did.

Agents located the two entertainers in another city and obtained a description of the man who was with them in Albany. They didn't know his name and said he had joined them simply as one of their admirers.

Back in Albany the agents talked with the girl who had been given the torn money. She described the man and said that he had talked a lot about show business. She had the impression that he was some kind of actors' agent.

Armed with this information and the man's description, agents interviewed several theatrical agents in New York. Gradually they narrowed their search to a man who had managed various entertainers and who lived in Brooklyn. We'll call him Forster, which isn't his real name.

The agents found Forster and listened to his story. While on a business trip to Albany he had won more than a thousand dollars in a crap game and went on a drinking spree. He had only a dim recollection of tearing three $100 bills in half and giving portions to some girl. Next morning he found three halves of $100 bills in his pockets. He gave these to Spence, who was his accountant, and told Spence that if the pieces were worth anything, Spence could apply the amount to Forster's account.

Now the agents brought Spence and Forster together and questioned Spence once more. Spence admitted that Forster had given him the pieces of the notes, but insisted that the burnt edges must have occurred in the accident involving his car.

"That's impossible," the agents told him. "Your car wasn't burned in any way. And the police are still holding the papers that were in your glove compartment."

"Well—uh—then my little nephew must have burned the edges, as I said. I thought there were three whole bills in the envelope, but I guess there were only the three pieces."

"That story just doesn't hold water," the agents said. "Your affidavit states that you had three whole bills to begin with. And now you admit that Mr. Forster gave you three torn halves."

Forster spoke up. "Say, Spence, I wonder if it couldn't be that you had these pieces near an ashtray on your desk, and maybe they were burned by a lighted cigarette?"

Spence acted puzzled. "That could be," he said. "Yes, I think maybe that's what happened."

The agents informed Spence of his constitutional rights and placed him under arrest. He was charged with making a false affidavit and a false claim against the Government, and also for the fraudulent mutilation of the $100 bills. After he was indicted, Spence pleaded not guilty, then changed his plea to guilty and was sentenced to pay a fine of $1,000 and to pay the cost of the prosecution. Because it was his first criminal offense, he was not sent to prison.

This is only one of many cases in which greedy people try to cheat the Treasury with mutilated money. On the other hand, there are numerous instances involving people who have accidents resulting in damage to paper money, and who make legitimate claims for refunds. The Treasury has redeemed money that has been gnawed by mice, torn in laundries, decayed after long burial in the earth, ruined by chemicals, chewed by children, and partially burned by accident. But any person who mutilates money with an intent to defraud is, upon conviction, liable for a severe fine and imprisonment.

Paper money that has been *partly* burned might be redeemable. If, however, the money has been completely reduced to ashes, it's as worthless as scorched paper towels.

If you find or own mutilated paper money, you may learn whether or not it has value by sending it to the Currency Redemption Division, Treasury Department, Washington, D.C. 20220. But whatever you do, *don't send ashes!*

Frauds involving mutilated money are not uncommon, but they are few when compared to a multimillion-dollar racket also investigated by the Secret Service—namely, the theft, forgery and fraudulent cashing of United States Treasury checks.

Chapter 9

THE CHECK THIEVES

When she was a little girl, Marian was a real tomboy. She dressed in boys' clothing whenever she could. She was the only girl on the neighborhood boys' baseball team. Later she was also the only girl who was an active member of "The Tigers," a youthful gang of petty thieves. She was arrested twice and released on probation as a juvenile. From stealing fruit, candy, perfume and similar goods, Marian graduated to the "big time." She began to forge and cash stolen checks.

At first she stole blank checks from stores and banks and made them out in fictitious names. In one store she took not only 162 checks, but also a "check protector," a device used to keep checks from being altered or forged. She traveled through Virginia, North Carolina, West Virginia and Kentucky, forging and cashing the stolen checks.

Then she made a bigger mistake. She began to steal United States Treasury checks from house mailboxes. These checks were made payable to people for Social Security benefits, income tax refunds, pensions and other purposes.

Ordinarily, it would seem difficult for a woman to steal a check made out to "John Jones" and try to cash it by saying that she was "John Jones." But this didn't bother tomboy Marian at all. She had a mannish haircut, and whenever she stole a check bearing the name of a man, she dressed in men's clothing and posed as the owner of the check.

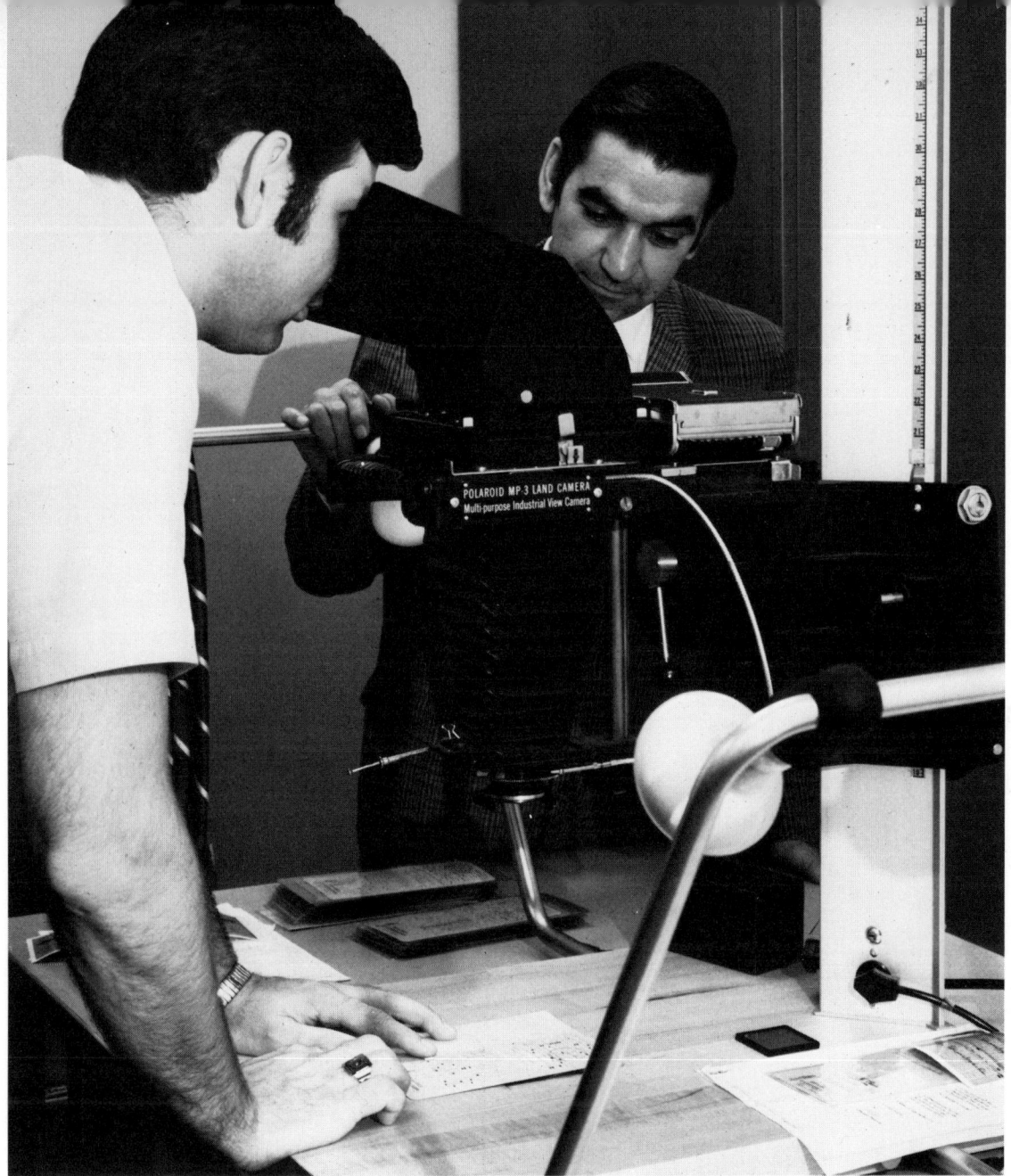
Filtered photographs help "remove" bank stamps which appear over forged endorsements on checks.

In one Virginia bank Marian cashed a stolen Treasury check payable to a woman. She left the bank, disguised herself as a man, then went right back to the same bank and cashed another check made out to a man.

When some of the stolen Treasury checks came to the Secret Service for investigation, they were examined in the Secret Service crime laboratory. Experts there developed fingerprints on the checks. From previous arrests, the fingerprints were identified as Marian's, and agents began to track her down.

The trail of stolen checks led from town to town and indicated that Marian could be heading gradually toward her parents' home in Virginia. Agents kept the house under observation. One night Marian drove up in a rented automobile and was arrested as she carried a suitcase toward the front door. In the suitcase agents found seven stolen Treasury checks and a number of stolen blank commercial checks. They also found some of the men's clothing she used as a disguise.

Marian was convicted and sentenced to serve five years in a Federal prison.

In another case a man and wife, Paul and Sharon, stole more than two hundred Treasury checks from house mailboxes and by breaking into private homes. Paul made counterfeit drivers' licenses and other documents to use for identification in cashing the checks.

In addition to the checks, the couple also stole automobiles.

Secret Service agents finally obtained a photograph of Paul, taken at the time of an earlier arrest. They sent copies of the picture to numerous banks, along with a warning to put banks on the alert for the couple.

One day Paul tried to cash a forged Treasury check at a drive-in bank in Richmond, Virginia. The lady teller was not satisfied with his identification and refused to cash the check.

Paul drove away, but not before the teller wrote down the license number of the Cadillac convertible he used. The teller then remembered the Secret Service warning and pulled it from the files. The picture was that of the man who drove the Cadillac.

The teller called the Secret Service. Agents sped to the vicinity of the bank and found the Cadillac in a parking lot not far away. They waited. When a man approached and got into the car he was arrested. He said that he and his wife were living in a tent in a nearby state park, and within half an hour the agents also took Sharon into custody.

The Cadillac had been stolen from a car dealer in Maryland.

Both Paul and Sharon pleaded guilty to the thefts and forgeries of Treasury checks in various parts of the United States. Paul was sentenced to serve twenty-five years and Sharon to ten years in prison.

Every year the United States Government sends out some 600 million Treasury checks. They go to war veterans, old-age pensioners, families of men in the armed forces, farmers, Federal employees and Social Security beneficiaries, among others. Many are poor people who depend heavily upon the checks to buy food, pay rent, and for other living expenses.

And every year thieves steal some fifty thousand or more of these checks from private homes and apartment houses. Most of the stolen checks are cashed by retail storekeepers who fail to ask for positive identification of the persons with the checks.

One merchant cashed a stolen check presented by a twelve-year-old boy, even though the printing on the check disclosed that it had been issued for "Old Age and Survivors Insurance."

Sometimes check thieves follow mail-carriers on their routes on the third day of each month, when many Government checks are usually delivered. The carriers drop the checks in mailboxes and within a few minutes the thieves pull them out, forcing open the boxes if they have to.

Frequently the thieves also take other mail, such as gas, electric or telephone bills that are addressed to the owners of the checks. In trying to cash the checks, the thieves produce the other mail to serve as identification. In some cases they have even paid the bills with the checks, obtaining the balance in cash.

Numerous Government checks are stolen by drug addicts who need as much as a hundred dollars a day or more to buy drugs.

Every year the Secret Service arrests two to three thousand check thieves and forgers. Sadly enough, about fifteen in every hundred are boys and girls under twenty years of age.

Many of these arrests could be avoided if storekeepers would insist upon getting proper identification of strangers who want to cash Government checks. A Social Security card, for instance, is *not* good identification, because it is issued only for Social Security purposes. In fact, the card includes the printed warning, "For Social Security Purposes—Not For Identification." Yet merchants often accept such cards as proof of identity in cashing stolen checks.

Some storekeepers think it's a waste of time to ask for identification when a stranger asks them to cash a Government check, because they think that a Government check is as good as gold. It is—but only if it's endorsed and cashed by its rightful owner. If it has been stolen and forged, it's as worthless as fool's gold.

There are precautions we can take to protect ourselves against becoming victims of check thieves. For instance, if your family receives or expects to receive Government checks:

1. Some member of the family should try to be at home when checks are due to be delivered. Checks should be taken from the mailbox as soon as possible.
2. The mailbox should be kept locked. If the box doesn't have a lock, get one.
3. No check should be endorsed until its owner is in the presence of the person who will cash it.
4. The payee (owner) of monthly checks should try to cash them in the same place each month, to make identification easier; preferably in a bank.

Handwriting characteristics on forged checks are studied, analyzed and compared with the handwriting specimens of suspected forgers.

Perhaps your family owns a store or business where customers ask that Government checks be cashed. If so, the owner of the business should:

1. Insist that a stranger who presents a Government check identify himself properly as the rightful owner of that check. The best way is to have the stranger vouched for by someone the storekeeper knows and considers reliable.
2. Ask himself this question: "IF THIS CHECK IS FORGED, CAN I FIND THE FORGER AND RECOVER MY LOSS?" (The merchant who accepts a forged Treasury check is the loser.)
3. Insist that all checks be endorsed as he looks on.
4. Put his initials on all checks and make a note on each check describing the kind of identification used.

With thousands of Government checks being stolen and forged, another kind of thief and forger is making more and more work for the Secret Service. This is the man or woman who steals, forges and cashes United States Savings Bonds. . . .

Chapter 10

THE FORGED BOND RACKET

In Memphis, Tennessee, a fat man walked into a bank and wanted to exchange $2,000 in U.S. Savings Bonds for cash. Asked for identification, he produced a New York State chauffeur's license that bore his photograph. The name on the license was the same as that on the bonds.

The bank teller asked the man for more identification.

"I left my credit cards and some other papers back at the hotel," the man said. "I'll go get them and come right back."

He walked away hurriedly, leaving the bonds and the license. The teller became suspicious and called the Secret Service. He furnished the bond numbers, and the Secret Service records showed that these bonds had been stolen by a burglar from the home of a retired railroad worker in Flushing, New York.

Immediately the Secret Service telephoned other Memphis banks and learned that a man of the same description had already cashed a number of bonds. Although agents staked out the one bank, the suspect did not return for the bonds he had left.

The chauffeur's license he used was found to be counterfeit. From small bits of information that the man had dropped in talking with bank officials, agents in New York were able to establish that he had been employed there as a butcher. They also discovered that he had moved to Opa Locka, Florida, where he was working in a market.

In Opa Locka, agents went to the market and arrested the butcher, who said he knew nothing about any stolen or forged bonds. He admitted that the counterfeit license carried his photograph, but insisted that someone else had used it.

Back in Memphis, the Secret Service picked up 41 stolen bonds that had been cashed by Memphis banks. The laboratory experts succeeded in bringing out a number of fingerprints on the bonds, and some of these proved to be those of the butcher. Faced with this evidence, the man confessed that the bonds had been stolen by two other men who forced him to forge and cash them.

The two other men were arrested in Little Rock, Arkansas, where they were convicted and sentenced. The butcher was convicted in Memphis and sent to prison for five years.

In these days of a growing crime rate, many house burglars make a specialty of stealing U.S. Savings Bonds. One such thief was known as "Funeral Ben" because he always read the obituary columns in newspapers, noting the days on which funerals would be held. Then, while families were attending the funerals, Ben broke into their homes and searched for savings bonds.

Like other professional burglars, Ben knew all the customary hiding places. Householders kept bonds in bureau drawers, in shoe boxes, under mattresses, in cookie jars, vases, bookshelves and other "secret" strongholds.

One drawback with such hiding places is that a family may not discover that its bonds are missing until months after a robbery. If an emergency brings a sudden need for the bonds, they may not be readily available and it may be some time before replacements are made.

Good Secret Service work led to the arrests of two men and a woman who stole a small fortune in savings bonds belonging to Mrs. Ella Ware (that's not her real name) in Louisiana. Unfortunately, Mrs. Ware had hidden the bonds at home instead of putting them in a safe-deposit box in a bank.

The robber trio cashed $17,000 worth of the bonds in New Orleans before the owner notified the Secret Service that the bonds had been stolen. The Secret Service in New Orleans obtained descriptions of the three thieves, who had mentioned to bank officials that they were driving west. The descriptions were sent to Secret Service offices in Texas.

An agent in Waco, Texas, immediately notified banks in that area to be on the alert for anyone trying to cash savings bonds payable to

Ella Ware. One bank reported that it had already cashed $3,000 worth for a woman whose description was the same as that broadcast by the Secret Service.

In San Antonio the Secret Service rushed descriptions to all San Antonio banks and to local motels, asking that the Secret Service be notified if anyone tried to cash Ella Ware bonds, or if anyone answering the descriptions of the trio checked in at any motel.

The very next day a San Antonio motel manager notified the Secret Service that a man and woman fitting the descriptions had checked in, registered as Mary and Adam Brown, brother and sister.

Agents went to the motel and took up watch in a room from which they could observe the two rooms occupied by the suspected pair. They also questioned a chambermaid who had serviced those rooms.

"I did see something interesting," the maid said. "In the woman's room I saw her take some clothes out of a suitcase, and a great big roll of bills fell on the floor. It must have been about four inches thick!"

The Browns had given a New York address on the motel register. Telephone calls to the Secret Service in New York revealed that Mary and Adam Brown were unknown at that address.

The following day agents saw a taxi drive up to the motel. A man got out and went to Adam Brown's room. The passenger answered the description of the third thief.

Agents checked with the taxi company and learned that the man had been picked up at the San Antonio International Airport and had been driven directly to the motel. He had no luggage.

In the afternoon Adam Brown came out of his room, went to the parking area and drove away in a Chevrolet sedan. A check of the license disclosed that it was a car rented in Dallas.

In Dallas, agents found that the car had been rented to a woman fitting the description of Mary Brown, accompanied by a man. As identification, she had furnished a New York State driver's license in the name of Josephine Sharpe. Josephine Sharpe was the name of the owner of a stack of savings bonds stolen from a bank in Key West, Florida, months earlier.

Dallas agents also discovered that the car renter had attempted to cash a number of bonds in a Dallas bank, but had failed because a bank officer was not satisfied with her identification.

Secret Service agents in Austin, Texas, brought bank employees to San Antonio, where they were taken to a room at the motel from which they could see the woman and two men. They positively identified the woman as the person for whom they had cashed savings bonds in the name of Ella Ware.

Agents now obtained arrest and search warrants for the three suspects and entered their rooms. The woman rushed to the bathroom and threw an envelope into the toilet bowl. An agent quickly retrieved it. The envelope contained $15,400 in $5, $10, $20, $50 and $100 bills, and a bank strap marked with a number and date. The number identified a teller at the Austin bank where the Ella Ware bonds had been cashed.

In a suitcase in Mary Brown's room the agents found fifty-four $1,000 savings bonds payable to Ella Ware. A key carried by Mary Brown fitted the lock on this suitcase.

The two men refused to talk, but Mary Brown admitted that she forged and cashed bonds in Austin, Dallas, and Waco, Texas, and in New Orleans, Louisiana.

In court, Mary Brown pleaded guilty and involved ten men and two other women in the wholesale theft and forgery of savings bonds. She received a suspended sentence of five years, but the men arrested with her were sent to jail for four and five years, and fined $5,000 each.

Ella Ware, from whom the fortune in bonds was stolen, did not lose her money, because U.S. Savings Bonds are safer to hold than cash. If you should lose a $20 bill, you've simply lost $20. But if you own a $100 savings bond that is stolen, lost or destroyed, the Treasury Department will replace that bond after the Secret Service has made an investigation of the circumstances.

The Secret Service has some good advice for people who buy and hold savings bonds:

1. Keep your bonds in a safe-deposit box in a bank or in some other equally safe place.
2. Keep a record of the serial numbers, amounts and dates of issue; and keep this record in a separate place—*not* with the bonds.
3. If your bonds are stolen, lost or destroyed, use your list to send the bond numbers, issue dates and denominations, with the name and address of the registered owner (the name that appears on the bonds) to the Division of Loans and Currency, Treasury Department, 536 South Clark Street, Chicago, Illinois 60605.

Thefts of savings bonds are extensive. In a single year thieves stole nearly $1,125,000 worth—mostly from homes and other places where the owners thought their bonds were safely hidden.

Tracking down the bond thieves is only one job of the Secret Service special agent, who gets special training for this and the many other law-enforcement duties he performs.

Chapter 11

THE SECRET SERVICE AGENT

Want to be a special agent of the Secret Service? You could be, if you're at least 21 years old and in good health physically and mentally, and have excellent eyesight. But that's not all. You must also:
1. Be a college graduate, preferably having completed courses in police science, police administration, or criminology. Special consideration is given to graduates who have maintained a "B" average or who graduate in the top 25 per cent of their class.
2. Pass a U.S. Civil Service written examination to test your observation and memory, your arithmetical reasoning, your clarity in writing, your vocabulary, and your ability to interpret statements. If you pass with a grade of 70 or better, you will be interviewed and rated on such factors as your personal appearance, bearing, and manner; your ability to speak logically and effectively; and your adaptability to group situations.

If you're favorably considered for appointment, you will first be the subject of a thorough investigation into your honesty, integrity, general character, and loyalty to the United States.

If you are offered an appointment, you should keep in mind the fact that if you accept it you must take part in raids, keep suspects and buildings under observation, make arrests, be assigned to protective duties, and perform other law-enforcement work that may be dangerous.

Incidentally, few Secret Service agents have been killed in the line of duty, although a large number have found themselves in hazardous situations.

One agent who gave his life was assigned to protect President Theodore Roosevelt, who visited Pittsfield, Massachusetts, in 1902 to make a speech. After the talk, the President planned to go to nearby Lenox. He and his secretary rode in a four-horse carriage with the Governor of Massachusetts and Secret Service Agent William Craig.

As the Presidential carriage drove down the main street, a trolley car carrying a few prominent citizens sped forward from one end of town, intending to reach Mr. Roosevelt's next stop before he did. The President's carriage at one point had to cross the trolley tracks. As it did so, the onrushing trolley kept coming and failed to slow down. Agent Craig jumped to his feet in the moving carriage and waved frantically as a signal for the car to stop. Moments later the speeding trolley crashed into the carriage, which was overturned. Craig was thrown into the air. The President and other passengers fell out and were shaken but not seriously hurt. Mr. Roosevelt rushed to Craig, who lay still. He was dead.

In another dramatic episode, Agent Robert Webster in 1927 was assigned to proceed from his headquarters in Florida to the island of Bimini to investigate reports that a counterfeiting plant was in operation there. He was given transportation on a Coast Guard vessel that patrolled the coast, watching for rum-runners. On the way to Bimini the Coast Guard ship hailed a small boat suspected of carrying alcohol illegally. The boat was searched and was found to contain a load of contraband whiskey. Its crew was placed under arrest.

One of the smugglers shot and killed the Coast Guard commander and wounded a member of the Coast Guard crew. Horace Alderman, another smuggler, then held Agent Webster and the other seaman at bay with his gun, and his men prepared to sink the patrol boat.

Alderman told his crew that he intended to kill Webster and the others so they couldn't testify against him. For just an instant, Alderman took his eyes off Webster to look into the engine room of the rum boat. In that fatal second, Webster leaped upon the man. Alderman fired one shot, killing Webster. Then he fired again at one of the Coast Guardsmen, who was hit and fell overboard (he was later rescued). At the same time, the other Coast Guardsmen fell upon Alderman, and one stabbed him with an ice pick. One grabbed Alderman's gun and rounded up his accomplices. Alderman was later convicted and executed for murder in the first degree.

In another case, in 1907, two Secret Service agents of the Denver District and a Bureau of Mines engineer investigated the theft of coal from Government land. While one agent and the engineer lowered them-

Even during William Howard Taft's administration (1909-1913), most of the men on foot around the President's carriage were Secret Service agents.

selves down a deep mine-shaft by a rope, the other agent remained on the surface to keep watch.

The two at the bottom of the shaft crawled through a long tunnel leading to an area where the coal had been removed. When they returned, they found the rope cut and the top of the shaft covered over. By arduously bracing both feet against the sides of the shaft, the agent slowly made it to the top and pulled up the engineer.

The agent they had left as lookout was nowhere in sight. In a search of the heavy brush they found his body. Agent Joseph Walker had been shot in the back. His gun was in its holster. Later, the Secret Service arrested the killer, who freely admitted that he had done the shooting, claiming that he had not known that Walker was a Government agent and had considered him a trespasser. He claimed that Agent Walker had threatened him with a revolver, and said he had shot Walker in the stomach in self-defense. The killer was indicted for first-degree murder. When the case was tried, a jury of cattlemen ignored the fact that Walker was shot in the back. They deliberated for twenty minutes and returned a verdict of not guilty.

Tragedies such as these have fortunately been rare in the Secret Service, but they are always remote possibilities that the agent must anticipate and try to avoid.

Don't get the idea that an agent's work is always exciting. Frequently it involves the tedious searching of files, interviewing people, walking the streets, doing desk work, or performing other unglamorous tasks that border on drudgery.

As a special agent you must also expect to be stationed anywhere in the United States, to work irregular hours in all kinds of weather, and to do considerable traveling. You may be away from home for Christmas or during other holiday seasons, and circumstances might conceivably make it difficult or impossible for you to be at home for family emergencies.

These possibilities may pose problems for special agents with wives and children, yet a great many Secret Service men do have families and manage to live satisfying, happy and productive lives. Some of the older men who are in charge of field offices, or who have earned promotions and become members of the Director's staff, have been in the Secret Service for twenty-five or thirty years or longer. Gradually, however, they retire and make way for numerous promotions of their younger associates.

Let's suppose that you accept appointment. You will be given your official credentials—a Secret Service badge and a commission as special agent.

For about a hundred years the Secret Service badge was a five-pointed silver star bearing an intricate engraved design and the inscription U.S. SECRET SERVICE. In 1970, the design was changed. The new red, blue and gold badge is shield-shaped, surmounted by the figure of an eagle. The design of the original five-pointed star is in the center of the shield, and the words, "The Department of the Treasury," form a circle in the center of the star. Between the eagle and the top of the star are the words, "United States," and at the bottom of the shield, "Secret Service."

(Above) Design of the Secret Service badge in use from 1873 to 1971. (Right) Design of the Secret Service badge adopted in 1971.

The special agent's commission is a leather folder with a reproduction of the badge on the outside. Inside there is a photograph of the agent, his signature, and the signature of the Director. The commission carries the heading, "UNITED STATES SECRET SERVICE, TREASURY DEPARTMENT," with the printed name and title of the holder, and the following authority:

> JOHN JONES
> Special Agent
>
> is commissioned by the United States Secret Service, Treasury Department, to protect the President of the United States and others as authorized by statute; to detect and arrest any person violating Federal laws relating to coins, obligations and securities of the United States and foreign governments, and other laws administered by the Treasury Department; and in the performance of his duties, to arrest any person committing any offense against the United States. He has top secret clearance and is commended to those with whom he may have official business as worthy of trust and confidence.

Your first assignment as a special agent in training will be to report to a Secret Service field office, perhaps in or near your home area. There you will begin an on-the-job training program. You'll meet your fellow

Firearms training for agents includes shooting from a moving vehicle.

agents, other Federal enforcement officers, police officials, and Government prosecutors. You'll sit in courtrooms and observe trials, knowing that before long you will be testifying as a prosecution witness in criminal cases.

You'll be taught the safe and proper use of guns. After you *prove* that you have learned how to shoot a revolver accurately and how to use it safely, a weapon will be issued to you. You will be required to practice with your gun at set intervals and to maintain required qualifying scores in target shooting.

After a short time in the field office, you will be sent to the Treasury Law Enforcement Officers School in Washington, D.C., for an intensive seven-week course. This course is given to agents of all of the Treasury Enforcement Agencies, which are:

    The U.S. Secret Service
    The Bureau of Customs
    The Alcohol, Tobacco Tax and Firearms Division, Internal
      Revenue Service
    The Intelligence Division, Internal Revenue Service

Draw-and-shoot practice on the pistol range.

Here are some of the subjects you will study in this school:

    Orientation to the Treasury Department
    Constitutional Law
    Firearms Training
    Ethics for Federal Investigators
    Evidence
    Photography
    Federal Court Procedures
    Fingerprints
    Laws of Arrest, Search and Seizure
    Report Writing
    Interviewing Techniques

After completing the seven-week course, you will return to the field office. There, during your first year, you must take a standard Red Cross course in first aid. If you can't swim, you must take a standard Red Cross swimming course. If you can swim, you must take an advanced course under the supervision of your Special Agent in Charge.

You must read certain books about criminal investigation on a required-reading list that is updated periodically.

You must read reports made by other agents on a variety of cases, and you must make a continuing careful study of the Secret Service Manual of Procedure, governing all aspects of Secret Service work. A copy of the manual will be part of your official equipment.

You will assist experienced agents as they conduct their investigations or make arrests.

An indoctrination course in handwriting characteristics will provide these men with important aspects of tracking down writers of threatening letters, forgers, and the like.

After some three months of this activity you will return to Washington to attend a Secret Service Training School. This school's courses cover specialized fields relating only to Secret Service duties. Among others, they include:

      Secret Service History and Jurisdiction
      Laws of Arrest, Search and Seizure
      Investigative Procedures
      Observation and Description
      Arrest Techniques
      Report Writing
      Firearms Training (revolver, shotgun, submachine gun)
      Interviewing Techniques
      Questioned Document Training (forgeries, handwriting, etc.)
      Production of Genuine Currency
      Detection of Counterfeit Currency
      Fundamentals and Techniques of Protection
      Human Behavior

After completing the Secret Service Training School course you will return to the field and complete your first year as a Secret Service Special Agent. During this first year you are on probation, and if in that time you

Secret Service agents are close at hand to protect the kin of Presidents. Above, President Richard M. Nixon's two daughters, Julie and Tricia, escorted by David Eisenhower and Edward Cox, are preceded and followed by men of the Secret Service.

have shown that you are not qualified or competent to perform your duties effectively, you may be released.

Your duties in the field may or may not be varied. For example, you could be assigned to work only on counterfeiting cases, or only on check- and bond-forgery cases. On the other hand, in an average week you might help to track down a counterfeiter, arrest a forger or forgers, try to find the writer of a letter threatening the life of the President, and spend time testifying in court. Also, whatever your tasks, you will devote some time to the writing of reports on your findings.

If you complete your probationary year satisfactorily, you might remain in the field for another year. Then you could be assigned to a protective detail at the White House or elsewhere, or to one of the headquarters divisions in Washington—or you might stay in the field. If you are assigned to the Presidential Protective Division, whose members protect the President and members of his family, you will ordinarily remain there for two years and will then be reassigned to duty in a field office.

After you have had more experience, you may be selected for the Supervisory Training Course, designed to develop prospective supervisors. With a few years' experience you will have an opportunity to become the Special Agent in Charge of a field office or a member of the administrative staff of the Director in Washington, such as an inspector.

Secret Service inspectors make periodic inspections of all field offices to make sure that the offices are administered efficiently and in compliance with established procedures. They examine files, review pending cases, and make sure that counterfeit money and other contraband being held as evidence is properly secured. They talk with Federal judges, United States Attorneys, and with representatives of other law-enforcement agencies in the area. They conduct personal interviews with the special agents in charge and with the agents and clerks assigned to each office. Detailed inspection reports are submitted to the Director with the inspectors' recommendations and comments, and copies of the reports are furnished to the special agents in charge who are affected.

Whether you are an inspector, a special agent or a supervisor, you may be assigned to take part in programs aimed at improving your knowledge of modern law-enforcement methods, including managerial and executive responsibilities. You may be sent to certain universities, civil-service schools or other educational institutions for special job-related courses to broaden your horizons and to increase your opportunities for advancement and your value to the Secret Service.

As a special agent in training you will receive an excellent starting salary. You will get a raise in pay after your first six months and another at the end of your probationary year. Civil-service salary figures have been increased by Congress in recent years and are not specified here because any dollar-amounts may be obsolete by the time this book is printed. Raises in pay are automatic, and you will be entitled to splendid fringe benefits such as sick leave, vacation time, and low-rate hospital and life insurance.

Also, as a special agent, you will be able to retire on a good pension at the minimum age of fifty, if you have twenty years of service or more. You would not be too old at that age to try another career, if you want to, or to set up a business of your own. One former agent became a vice-president of the American Express Company. One was hired as Director of Security for the United States Banknote Company. One is a security consultant for the Board of Governors of the Federal Reserve System, and another is Chief of Security for The Greenbriar, a famous resort hotel. Some former agents are self-employed private investigators—and many simply draw their pensions and spend time with their families, travel, or pursue a variety of hobbies.

All in all, a career as a Secret Service agent is well worth whatever time and work you may spend on your educational program to plan for it. As one agent said when he was assigned to protect the President, "I never thought I'd get to the White House, but I've made it, after all!"

Chapter 12

MISSION: PROTECTION

President Abraham Lincoln was shot and killed in 1865 by John Wilkes Booth, a fanatical actor who hated Lincoln for freeing the slaves and blamed him for the defeat of the Confederacy. Lincoln was the first U.S. President to be assassinated, although in 1835 there had been an unsuccessful attempt to kill one of his predecessors, Andrew Jackson.

Mr. Jackson was attending a funeral in the Capitol in Washington. After the services, as he and some of his friends walked down the hall past a crowd of mourners, an excited man plowed his way through the crowd and dashed toward the President.

Before anyone could stop him, the assailant thrust a pistol against the President's chest and pulled the trigger. The gun failed to fire.

Instantly, the man drew a second pistol, pointed it at Jackson, and again pulled the trigger. The hammer clicked, but there was no shot.

By this time the President and his friends had leaped upon the attacker, who was turned over to local police. Both of the pistols were test-fired over and over—and there was not a single misfire! The amazed firearms experts concluded that a miracle had occurred and that Mr. Jackson must have had an alert guardian angel.

In 1881, after James A. Garfield was elected President, he received letters from Charles Guiteau, a religious fanatic, demanding that the President appoint him American Consul in Paris, France. The President passed the letters on to the Secretary of State, who told Guiteau that the Consular post in Paris was already filled.

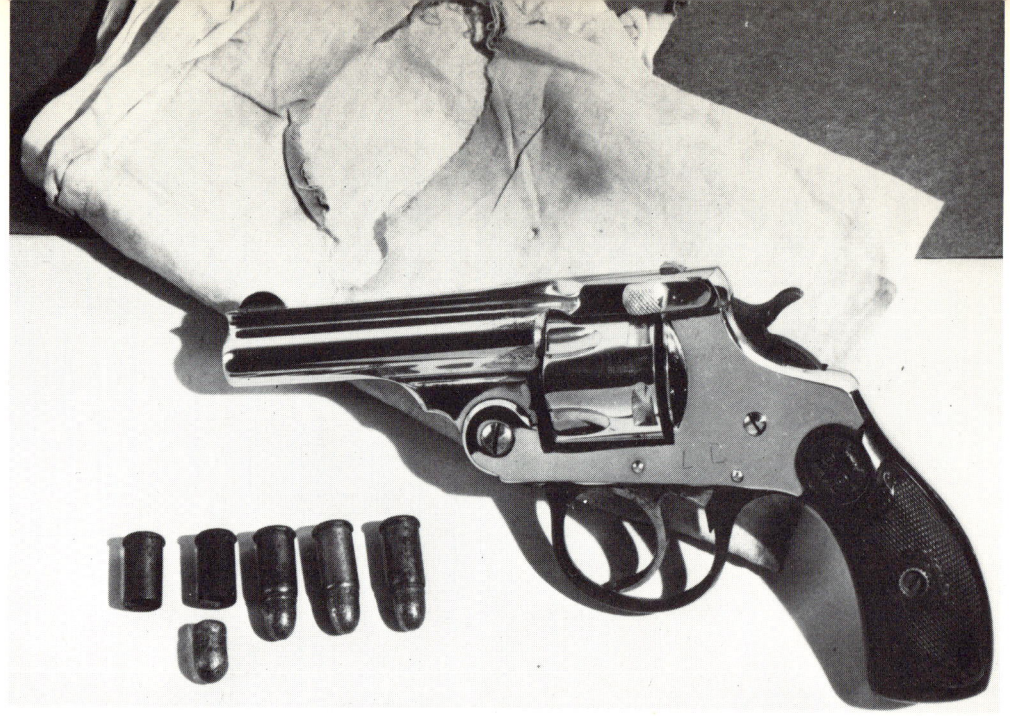

Pictured here is the .32-caliber Ivor Johnson revolver used by assassin Leon Czolgosz when he shot President William McKinley in Buffalo, N.Y., on September 6, 1901.

Guiteau kept sending impossible demands to the President and the State Department, and finally came to believe that God had commanded him to "remove" the President. He bought a revolver and practiced shooting with it.

On several occasions Guiteau had the opportunity to shoot Mr. Garfield, but failed to do so until one day when he read that the President was preparing to leave Washington. At the Washington railroad station Guiteau watched the President walk past him. Then he drew his revolver and shot Garfield twice in the back. He immediately surrendered to a police officer and demanded protection from the outraged spectators.

The President died several weeks later and Guiteau was convicted of the murder and executed.

Next in the assassination field was Leon Czolgosz, an anarchist who believed that all rulers should be killed. In 1901 Czolgosz shot and killed President William McKinley as the latter stood shaking hands with well-wishers in a receiving line in Buffalo, New York.

Only after this tragedy did Congress authorize the U.S. Secret Service to protect McKinley's successors. Up to that time there was no provision for any formal or official protection for the occupant of the White House.

On February 15, 1932, President-elect Franklin D. Roosevelt spoke before a large crowd in Bay Front Park, Miami, Florida. After the talk, as Mr. Roosevelt sat in his open car, he was approached by Anton Cermak, then Mayor of Chicago. Mr. Cermak stood close to the automobile, chatting and smiling. In the midst of the throng a mentally ill Italian immigrant, Giuseppe Zangara, jumped up on a chair, pointed a revolver at the car and fired five shots.

One bullet grazed the hand of a Secret Service agent and struck Mayor Cermak. The others hit four more spectators, including a New York police detective. Mr. Roosevelt was unharmed, but Mr. Cermak died in the hospital.

Some people, including newspapermen, raised a question as to whether Zangara intended to kill the Mayor or the President-elect. When he was questioned, Zangara made it clear that he wanted to kill Mr. Roosevelt, whom he held responsible for severe stomach pains.

Zangara was executed the month after the shooting.

Another assassination attempt was made November 1, 1950, in Washington, D.C., by two Puerto Ricans who tried to shoot their way into Blair House, which was then used as a temporary residence by President and Mrs. Harry S. Truman (see Chapter 13).

President John F. Kennedy was the first American President to be killed since the Secret Service was assigned the task of protecting Presidents. The circumstances of his assassination were such that it would have been virtually impossible to have prevented the tragic shooting (see Chapter 1).

Since 1901 the Federal law defining the duties of the Secret Service has been broadened several times, and by 1971 these duties were set out in Title 18 of the U.S. Code of Laws, Section 3056, which authorizes the Secret Service:

> To protect the President of the United States and members of his immediate family; the President-elect; the Vice-President or other officer next in the order of succession to the Office of the

Secret Service agents, alternating between walking and riding, provided protection for President Franklin D. Roosevelt while the President visited Des Moines, Iowa, on September 4, 1936.

Watchful agents stay close to the Chief Executive at large public events.

President; the Vice-President-elect; a former President and his wife during his lifetime; the widow of a former President until her death or remarriage; minor children of a former President until they reach sixteen years of age; persons who are determined from time to time by the Secretary of the Treasury, after consultation with an advisory committee, as being major Presidential or Vice-Presidential candidates who should receive such protection (unless the candidate has declined such protection).

To detect and arrest offenders for counterfeiting the coins, currency, stamps and other obligations and securities of the United States.

To suppress forgery and fraudulent negotiation of Government checks, bonds, and other obligations or securities of the United States.

To conduct investigations relating to certain criminal violations of the Gold Reserve Act of 1934; the Silver Purchase Act; the Federal Deposit Insurance Act; the Federal Land Bank Act; the Home Owners Loan Act; and the Government Losses in Shipment Act.

In 1970 Congress amended the law again to give the Secret Service added security responsibilities once borne by the Department of State. Besides its other protective functions, the Secret Service is also authorized to "protect the person of a visiting head of a foreign state or foreign government and, at the direction of the President, other distinguished foreign visitors to the United States and official representatives of the United States performing special missions abroad...."

In other words, in addition to all other duties authorized by law, the 1970 amendment provides that the Secret Service will protect the persons of foreign monarchs, prime ministers, and (if the President so directs) foreign visitors such as political leaders or emissaries, and their U.S. counterparts going abroad. Supervision of this responsibility is the task of the Foreign Dignitary Protective Division of the Secret Service.

Under the law, all Federal agencies must support Secret Service protective missions when called upon by the Director, unless such authority is revoked by the President.

The agents who safeguard the President and the other distinguished people mentioned in the law are under the supervision of the Office of Protective Forces, which also oversees the Executive Protective Service (EPS). The latter is a uniformed security force that protects the White House and its grounds and the properties of foreign embassies and missions in the United States (see Chapter 13).

Since any Secret Service special agent may be assigned to protective duties, all agents undergo special security training as part of the courses in the Secret Service Training School. They learn how to make advance arrangements to protect the President, Vice-President, or other important official when he plans a journey at home or abroad. They practice the driving of the Presidential limousines under varying conditions. They make "dry runs" in which agents stand on special steps aboard the Secret Service car that always follows the President's automobile, and they learn how and when to jump from this moving "follow-up" car to relieve agents who are on foot beside the President's vehicle.

(Below) Agents of the Secret Service receive comprehensive training in motorcade-security techniques. (Right) Executive Protective Service patrol checks security at the Embassy of Iran.

The automobiles used by the agents and by the President always attract attention, yet few people know the extent to which these cars have been specially equipped for Secret Service action.

The limousine used by the President is a 21-foot custom-built black Lincoln Continental with a glass roof. Among its many novel and necessary security and engineering features are:

> A public address system.
> A system that can transmit outside sounds into the closed interior.
> A rear bumper that folds down to serve as a platform for Secret Service agents.
> An adjustable hydraulic handrail at the rear of the car for use by Secret Service agents.
> Two-way communications systems.
> Separate heating and air-conditioning units for front and rear compartments.
> A clear glass enclosure over the passenger compartment. A detachable black vinyl cover can be fitted over the glass roof if desired. The driver's compartment has a steel roof covered with black vinyl.

(Top left) 1961 Lincoln Continental used by Presidents John F. Kennedy and Lyndon B. Johnson. (Bottom left) Oversized 1950 Lincoln used by President Harry S. Truman. When President Dwight D. Eisenhower took office, he requested the clear plastic roof so that the President could see and be seen in bad weather; this car then became known as the "bubbletop." (Below) The "Sunshine Special," a specially built 1939 Lincoln used by President Franklin D. Roosevelt.

The President's limousine has a regular rear seat and three rear-facing theater-type seats, permitting comfortable seating of six passengers.

A 40-watt fluorescent light in the rear compartment permits its passengers to be seen from the street at night.

When the President rides in the limousine, the flag of the United States is flown from the right fender and the President's standard from the left fender. The flags are illuminated at night by three miniature spotlights mounted on each fender.

The Seal of the President of the United States, a five-inch disc, is mounted on each side of the car on the center panel between the front and rear doors.

The car is powered by a 340-horsepower, 462-cubic-inch Lincoln Continental V-8 engine.

To accompany the Presidential limousine, the Secret Service uses two special Lincoln Continental black four-door convertibles with the latest security designs and equipment.

These cars are equipped with eleven-inch-wide running boards that extend the full length of the sides between front and rear wheel-cut openings. Handles and bars are installed to be grasped by agents who stand on the running boards.

The rear doors have been specially reworked to permit agents to enter the car from the running boards while the vehicle is moving. This was done by cutting the rear doors in half and reconnecting them to allow the front portion of the doors to slide over the rear half, creating a fifteen-inch walk-through. For normal entry, the rear doors will open and close in the customary way.

Across the rear of the car is an eleven-inch-wide retractable platform. A hinged "assist bar" mounted on the deck lid is operated hydraulically so it can be adjusted to the most convenient position for grasping when agents stand on the platform.

The Presidential limousine, operated and maintained by the U.S. Secret Service, incorporates the latest in security design and equipment.

The convertible tops of the Secret Service follow-up cars are of transparent vinyl to allow agents to observe rooftops and other tall structures.

The cars have special heavy-duty tires and wheels designed for heavy loads.

The divided front seats are modified so that a man may ride facing the rear on the center portion between the seats.

The cars are equipped with highly advanced electronic communication gear, public-address speakers, sirens, red emergency flasher lights, and special weapons for emergency use.

Making "dry runs" in the Lincoln follow-up car is only one phase of the training of agents. A different kind of study, for example, includes sessions at a government institution for the mentally ill.

The reason for such studies is that many people who threaten the President's life or who seek to harm him physically are not of sound mind. At the hospital the agents talk with specialists to learn how best to cope with victims of various forms of mental illness. This training is especially helpful to agents assigned to the Office of Protective Intelligence.

This OPI section supports the various protective units. It collects, evaluates, coordinates, stores and disseminates information that may be useful to agents on security assignments. The Office of Protective Intelligence maintains a Liaison Division that keeps in close touch with all major Government agencies to exchange information of interest to them or to the Secret Service.

The Office of Protective Intelligence has agents who are on duty day and night. Some are assigned to receive unusual or abusive telephone calls referred to them by operators at the White House switchboard. Others may be summoned by Executive Protective Service officers at the gates of the White House grounds to talk with strangers who come there and insist upon seeing the President.

Because agents on protective details must be prepared for any emergency, they take courses in fire fighting, judo, and other techniques of self-defense. They are exposed to tear gas in order to experience its effect. Firearms training includes special sessions in shooting at night. Agents also learn about different types of bombs.

The Secret Service has a "bomb carrier" of its own design—a motorized vehicle to transport explosive devices to selected isolated areas, if necessary. The vehicle is so designed that if a suspected bomb were to explode inside it while in transit, the explosion would inflict little or no damage upon nearby persons or property unless the bomb was extremely powerful.

In these days of international intelligence-gathering, the use of listening devices ("bugs") is well-known. The Secret Service has a Technical Security Division whose agents are trained to make electronic

Executive Protective Service officers check time of inspection at Japanese Embassy in Washington.

Open view of bomb carrier utilized by the U.S. Secret Service.

searches for such devices in so-called "sensitive" rooms. Details of equipment and techniques must obviously be kept secret.

This division also installs and services electronic alarms on windows and doors where necessary. It has a Technical Development and Planning Branch, staffed with electronic engineers. They keep abreast of the latest developments in the electronics world that may be of interest to the Secret Service in connection with its security work.

Agents of the Secret Service accompany Vice-President Spiro T. Agnew.

When the President or Vice-President travels, the Secret Service makes advance security arrangements for proper protection. An advance agent joins the Special Agent in Charge (SAIC) of the appropriate field office in making necessary studies, evaluations and preparations for the visit, including setting up an outer security perimeter. This means that advance teams survey the area to be visited by the President or other official, to decide what safety precautions will be required.

The advance team is also responsible for the placement and briefing of the people on protective assignments. These assignments are the primary responsibility of Secret Service agents who are brought to the center of action from many of the sixty-two field offices of the Service. Other advance arrangements include the selection of emergency sites, such as hospitals, routes of evacuation, and relocation areas.

The entire protective mission is controlled by a central command post that serves as a common vantage point and communications center. The command post receives and furnishes information pertinent to the job at hand.

Based upon the President's plans and wishes, agents talk with local and state police officials about routes of travel and assignments of police officers on streets and around buildings.

In addition to help from police on such occasions, the Secret Service is also assisted by the FBI and by agents from other Treasury enforcement units.

Secret Service agents inspect hotel or other rooms to be occupied by the President or Vice-President. Agents check on strangers who will have access to the area, including domestic servants and other hotel employees.

(Left) Agents with walkie-talkies assigned to special duties on the White House grounds. (Above) An old picture showing Secret Service agents guarding a shipment of currency being transferred from the Bureau of Engraving and Printing to the Treasury Building in Washington, D.C. The year: 1890.

At all times the agents on protective duties keep in close touch with each other and with the command post by walkie-talkie or by two-way car radios.

From time to time the Secret Service is assigned to special protective duties involving things rather than people. For example, in December, 1941, immediately following the Japanese bombing of Pearl Harbor, the Secret Service was chosen to safeguard priceless original historical documents. At night, its agents removed from the Library of Congress in Washington the Declaration of Independence, the Constitution of the United States, the Gutenberg Bible, Lincoln's Second Inaugural Address, and the Lincoln Cathedral Copy of the Magna Carta.* These treasures were sent by rail to the government vaults at Fort Knox, Kentucky, where they remained for the duration of World War II. At the war's end they were returned to Washington by the Secret Service.

In April, 1954, the Secret Service was assigned to protect the Charter of the United Nations when it was moved from San Francisco, California, to the State Department in Washington.

And in 1962-1963, Secret Service agents safeguarded Leonardo Da Vinci's priceless "Mona Lisa" portrait while it was on loan to the United States.

*Removal of the documents was supervised by the author of this book, Harry Edward Neal, then Executive Aide to the Chief of the Secret Service.

Security work is not easy. On one Presidential assignment, agents flew nonstop from California to Vietnam (twenty-six hours) and began their protective duties immediately. They worked from sixteen to twenty hours a day for three consecutive days, then returned nonstop to Washington and took up their regular duties with no time off.

James J. Rowley, Director of the Secret Service, has told Congress: "Our agents did not give in to physical discomforts, even though their actions were at times against medical advice. For example, some of their afflictions were diagnosed by physicians as pneumonia and complete physical exhaustion; some contracted intestinal disease in Vietnam. One suffered a fatal heart attack while he was making advance preparations for a candidate's visit. One doctor said that the symptoms he observed when examining some of our agents were the same as those he saw in combat fighter pilots—mental and physical exhaustion brought on by extremely prolonged periods of duty under constant tension."

Director Rowley added: "Our agents have been assaulted with fists, rocks, and one was injured by a moving automobile. Their clothing was frequently damaged. And, of course, the agents could not be at home for family births, deaths, illnesses and other emergencies."

A brief word must be said here about Secret Service participation in the training of Treasury Air Security Officers (TASO), popularly known as "sky marshals." These are the men assigned to fly as passengers aboard various aircraft, prepared to prevent the hijacking of planes, if possible.

When the sky marshal program began in 1970, agents from the Secret Service, the FBI, the Bureau of Narcotics and Dangerous Drugs, the Customs Bureau, Internal Revenue and other enforcement agencies were assigned to the program as a temporary emergency measure, until men could be recruited elsewhere for permanent assignment.

The recruiting is done by the Treasury Department's Bureau of Customs, which conducts the Treasury Air Security Officers School (TASOS) for training applicants. Representatives of various Federal bureaus take part in the instruction, which includes methods of interrogation; laws of arrest, search and seizure; handling of evidence; and so on. Training in the use and handling of firearms is provided by special agents of the Secret Service and is of the greatest importance, since most hijackers have used guns to force crews to fly to unscheduled destinations.

Note to potential plane hijackers: The odds on "getting away with it" are getting smaller all the time.

Agents who travel with the President, Vice-President or other officials are only a part of the group engaged in security work. Perhaps not many people realize that the Secret Service has two uniformed security forces specially trained for their unique and essential protective duties.

Chapter 13

GUARDIANS IN UNIFORM

About two o'clock in the afternoon of November 1, 1950, two Puerto Rican men walked along Pennsylvania Avenue in Washington toward Blair House. Government-owned Blair House is diagonally across the street from the White House, and because the White House was in the process of being renovated, President and Mrs. Harry S. Truman were living temporarily at Blair House.

One of the Puerto Ricans, Griselio Torresola, went toward the house from the west. The other, Oscar Collazo, approached from the east. At each corner of the house was a small wooden booth occupied by a uniformed officer of the White House Police Force, a unit of the Secret Service.

The west booth was manned by Officer Leslie Coffelt. Torresola had to pass this booth before he could reach the entrance to Blair House. He went to the open doorway of the booth as though to ask Coffelt a question. Without warning, Torresola yanked out an automatic pistol, aimed it point-blank at the officer, and fired. Three bullets hit Coffelt, who collapsed.

Just seconds before this tragedy unfolded, Oscar Collazo had passed the east police booth, where Officer Joseph C. Davidson was talking with Special Agent Floyd M. Boring of the White House Detail. Collazo mixed with several pedestrians on the sidewalk and paused in front of the steps leading to the Blair House doorway. Standing on the steps was White House Police Officer Donald T. Birdzell. Birdzell was turned

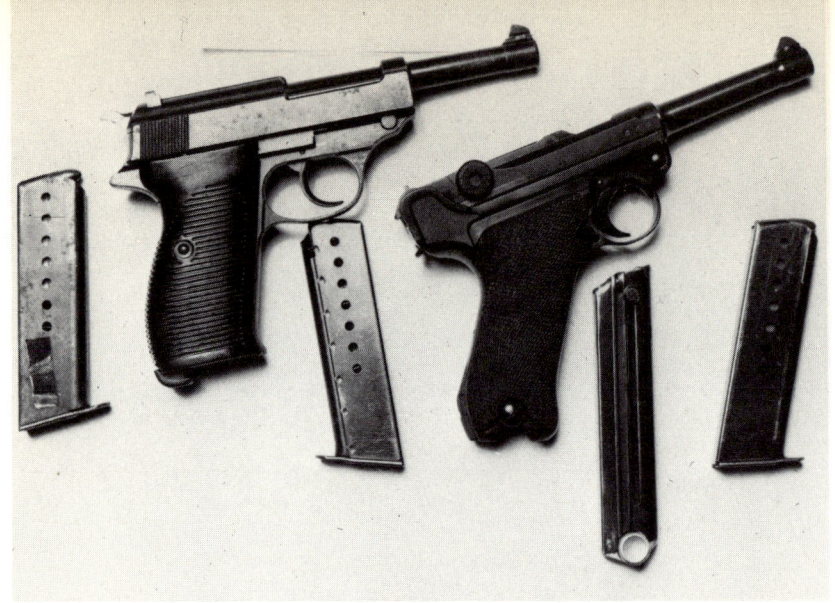

Weapons used by Oscar Collazo and Griselio Torresola on November 1, 1950, in their attempt to assassinate President Harry S. Truman at Blair House.

away from Collazo and didn't see him pull out a pistol. Collazo pointed it at the officer and pulled the trigger. The gun failed to go off, but Birdzell heard the click of the hammer just as Torresola shot Officer Coffelt at the west booth.

Birdzell turned quickly to see Collazo staring at the weapon in amazement. Birdzell drew his own revolver. Collazo tried again. This time his gun fired and a bullet struck Birdzell in one knee.

To draw Collazo's fire away from the building and the passers-by, Birdzell dashed into the road, firing at his attacker. Now Officer Davidson and Special Agent Boring opened fire on Collazo, who crouched on the Blair House steps, partially protected by the bars of an iron fence. Bullets struck the bars and whined as they ricocheted.

At the west booth Torresola tried to help Collazo. Torresola jumped the fence to the Blair House lawn. He shot at the wounded Birdzell in the road, hitting his other knee. Unable to stand, Officer Birdzell fell to the pavement.

Torresola saw another White House policeman, Joseph H. Downs, near the basement entrance to Blair House. He shot Downs three times.

In his booth, bleeding badly from his mortal wounds, Officer Leslie Coffelt managed to get outside his doorway. With a final Herculean effort he pulled his revolver, took careful aim, and killed Torresola with a single shot to the brain.

While all this was happening, President Truman appeared at a second-floor window of Blair House. Agent Boring yelled, "Get back! Get back!" The President withdrew from the window.

Collazo's ammunition gave out. With incredible calm he reloaded his gun, though he had been struck twice in the nose and ears. He stood up to shoot at Boring and Davidson. This time one of their bullets struck his chest and he slumped to the steps.

The gun battle lasted less than three minutes, during which time some twenty-seven shots were fired. Even if the two attackers had actually succeeded in entering Blair House, they would have been cut down instantly by a Secret Service agent posted at the foot of the main staircase with a submachine gun.

Officer Leslie Coffelt died, but Officers Birdzell and Downs recovered from their wounds.

Oscar Collazo was later sentenced to be executed, but his sentence was commuted to life imprisonment by President Truman.

A plaque at Blair House marks the scene and date of the gunfight and pays tribute to the bravery of Leslie Coffelt and members of the White House Police Force.

The White House Police Force grew from a small group of members of the Washington Police Department who were assigned in 1860 to safeguard the White House and its grounds. For many years these officers were responsible only to their Chief of Police and had no allegiance to the Secret Service, but in 1922, during the administration of President Warren G. Harding, Congress enacted a law establishing the "White House Police Force."

The Force was to be supervised by an officer designated by the President. President Harding named Colonel C. O. Sherrill, his chief military aide, and Sherrill in turn appointed Major O. M. Baldinger, the President's junior military aide, to supervise the Force.

In 1930 President Herbert Hoover decided that because the Secret Service was responsible for protection of the President, it should control all phases of Presidential protection. Upon his recommendation, Congress on May 14, 1930, gave supervision of the White House Police Force to the Chief of the Secret Service. (In 1970, Congress officially changed the title of "Chief" to "Director.")

The White House Police Force, as such, is no more. Under a law enacted March 19, 1970, its duties are now performed by members of the Executive Protective Service. This law says:

> "Subject to the supervision of the Secretary of the Treasury, the Executive Protective Service shall perform such duties as the Director, United States Secret Service, may prescribe in connection with the protection of the following:
> (1) the Executive Mansion and grounds in the District of Columbia; (2) any building in which Presidential offices are located; (3) the President and members of his immediate family; (4) foreign diplomatic missions located in the metropolitan area of the District of Columbia; and (5) foreign diplomatic missions located in such other areas in the United States, its territories and possessions, as the President, on a case-by-case basis, may direct."

An unobtrusive, but vigilant, Secret Service man is never far away from the President, even on a leisurely stroll.

The same law authorizes the employment of 850 members of the Executive Protective Service (EPS) and sets out the way in which they are to be recruited:

> "Members of the Executive Protective Service shall be recruited under the Civil Service laws and regulations on a nationwide basis. Members of such Service may also be appointed from the members of the Metropolitan Police force and the United States Park Police force from lists furnished by the officers in charge of such forces. Whenever any vacancy is created in the Metropolitan Police force or the United States Park Police force as the result of an appointment to the Executive Protective Service, such vacancy shall be filled in the manner provided by law. In the period of time which follows the date of enactment of this sentence [March 19, 1970] and precedes January 1, 1975, not more than thirty members of the Metropolitan Police force may be appointed annually to the Executive Protective Service."

To be appointed to the Executive Protective Service, a male applicant must meet Civil Service requirements. He must be a United States citizen between the ages of 21 and 29 years; be at least 5 feet 8 inches tall and not taller than 6 feet 4 inches, with weight in proportion; have a high school diploma or its equivalent; and have not less than 20/40 vision in each eye, correctable with glasses to 20/20. His starting pay will be $8,500 a year or more, depending upon Civil Service salary rates in effect at the time of his appointment.

On September 15, 1970, the first woman member of the EPS was appointed. She was Miss Phyllis Shantz of Rome, New York. Other women were later added to the EPS force. Some had previous experience as policewomen and were given on-the-job training in EPS. Those with no such experience participated in the EPS Recruit Training Course.

The physical requirements for EPS women applicants are rather flexible and somewhat similar to those for policewomen in the Washing-

Phyllis Shantz, first woman appointed to the Executive Protective Service, takes the oath of office. Officiating are (center) Mrs. Patricia R. Hitt, Assistant Secretary (Community and Field Services), Department of Health, Education and Welfare; and (right) Eugene T. Rossides, Assistant Secretary for Enforcement and Operations, Department of the Treasury.

ton Metropolitan Police Department. Their salaries and benefits are the same as those of other EPS officers.

Applications may be made to the U.S. Secret Service, 1800 G Street, N.W., Washington, D.C. 20226.

If he is appointed, the EPS officer will enter the Recruit Training Course to receive both classroom and on-the-job training for a twelve-week period. Among the subjects he will study in class are these:

> Organization and History of the Secret Service
> Self-defense and arrest tactics
> Use of Firearms
> First Aid
> Enforcement Law (District of Columbia and Federal laws, rules
>   of evidence, laws of search and seizure, and court procedures)
> Psychology for the Law-enforcement Officer
> Fire fighting
> Civil Disturbance Training

The new officer may be assigned to the EPS Foreign Missions Division, which protects foreign embassies and diplomatic missions, or to the EPS White House Division, responsible for the security of the White House and its grounds and the nearby Executive Offices Building.

EPS members wear distinctive police-type uniforms and specially designed badges. In addition to manning stationary duty posts, EPS officers drive blue automobiles with red roof-lights, and bearing on the car doors an image of the EPS badge with the words "Executive Protective Service Patrol." The patrol squads make frequent inspections of areas and buildings under EPS protection.

(Top left) Executive Protective Service officers communicate by means of two-way car radio. (Top right) Treasury Security Force officers at the Cash Room in the Treasury Building. (Right) Officers outside the Treasury Building.

The EPS is one of two uniformed security forces under Secret Service supervision. The other is the Treasury Security Force, formerly known as the Treasury Guard Force.

Officially the Treasury Security Force is within the jurisdiction of the General Services Administration (GSA) in Washington, but the GSA has formally authorized the Secretary of the Treasury to organize and maintain his own security group. In turn, the Secretary has delegated this authority to the Director of the Secret Service.

The Treasury Security Force has a man-sized responsibility, for it safeguards the billions of dollars in money and securities in the underground vaults of the Main Treasury Building, the nation's counting house.

The force also protects the Treasury Building itself, including the Cash Room that is used daily by the public. The Cash Room cashes large numbers of Treasury checks for government employees, exchanges paper money for coins (and vice versa), and transacts other financial business.

Officers of the Treasury Security Force are on constant alert in and near the Cash Room during business hours. Sometimes they are instrumental in arresting persons who attempt to cash stolen and forged Treasury checks there.

One morning, for instance, an officer on duty at the Cash Room noticed two men who had entered the building. One stood outside the Cash Room while the other went in and approached a teller's window, where he presented a Treasury check to be cashed. The check was already endorsed, but the teller asked the man to endorse it again. The man was so nervous that he found it difficult to write, and the teller correctly guessed that the endorsement was a forgery. The teller sounded a silent alarm. The alarm signal flashed in the office of the security force, and the signal identified the window at which it originated.

The officer at the Cash Room was instantly alerted. Since he had observed the two men come in together, he first arrested the one who had waited outside the room, then arrested the one who tried to cash the check. The officer called Secret Service agents, who took the pair into custody.

It developed not only that the check had been stolen and forged, but a search of the man who had waited in the hall also revealed thirty-two capsules of heroin concealed in his socks.

Both men were later convicted and sentenced.

In another Cash Room episode, a woman attempted to cash a forged check and was detained by the uniformed officers, who summoned agents. While awaiting arrival of the agents, the woman asked permission to visit the ladies' rest room. The security officers enlisted the services of a woman Treasury employee to first search the suspect. The search uncovered one pound of marijuana which she had hidden in her brassiere.

Treasury Security Force officers protect the nearby Treasury Annex as well as the Main Treasury Building. They are also posted outside the offices of the Secretary of the Treasury at all times for possible emergencies.

Like their EPS counterparts, the Treasury Security Force members undergo special training, including the handling and use of firearms. Many of the EPS and TSF officers are qualified as "Expert" with the revolver, and take great pride in displaying scores of trophies they have won in competition with some of the finest pistol shots in the world.

The Secret Service, too, is especially proud of its scores of agents who have reached the "Expert" level with revolvers and other firearms. Although the Secret Service stresses the importance of safety in the use of guns, it is aware that its agents may be compelled to use weapons as they go about their daily jobs of tracking down counterfeiters, forgers and other underworld characters.

In addition, in Secret Service field offices all over the country, agents continually investigate people who write letters threatening to kill the President, the Vice-President, or some other distinguished person receiving Secret Service protection.

Chapter 14

DON'T MAKE DEATH THREATS

The Secret Service receives and investigates thousands of Protective Intelligence cases every year. Some of these relate to people who have been heard to say they want to injure or kill the President or the Vice-President. Some involve writers of obscene letters. Others concern men and women whose letters threaten to kill the President or Vice-President for one reason or another.

Threats such as these are in violation of Federal law. If convicted, a person who makes a threat can be sent to prison for a long time.

The Federal law that applies in these cases reads in part this way:

> "Whoever knowingly and willfully deposits for conveyance in the mail or for a delivery from any post office or by any letter carrier any letter, paper, writing, print, missive, or document containing any threat to take the life of or to inflict bodily harm upon the President of the United States, the President-elect, the Vice-President or other officer next in the order of succession to the office of President of the United States, or the Vice-President-elect, or knowingly and willfully otherwise makes any such threat against the President, President-elect, Vice-President or other officer next in the order of succession to the office of President, or Vice-President-elect, shall be fined not more than $1,000 or imprisoned not more than five years, or both...."

Occasionally a man or woman openly declares that he or she intends to kill the President, and when questioned later, claims that the remark was made in jest. But there's nothing funny about an expressed intent to commit a murder, and the consequences can be serious.

In one case in New York City a nineteen-year-old boy we'll call Manuel bought an M-1 rifle and was asked by a co-worker what he intended to do with it.

"What do you think?" Manuel said. "Somebody has to follow in Oswald's footsteps. I'm going to shoot the President."

The co-worker reported the conversation by telephone to the Secret Service, but refused to identify himself. Agents arrested Manuel and learned that he was a member of a group of Fidel Castro sympathizers. In court he said, "I was only joking. I was going to use the gun to go hunting."

"Well," the judge said, "it was a tragic sort of joke, and I fail to appreciate any humor in it."

Manuel was sent to Bellevue Hospital for mental observation. Doctors there found that he was "not psychotic," so he was returned to court, given a suspended sentence and placed on probation for one year.

The Psychiatric Clinic of the Criminal Courts of the City of New York wrote to the Secret Service about Manuel. The Clinic's letter said, in part: "We conclude that you are prepared better for dealing with 'rational' motives than with 'irrational' ones, particularly when the latter appears as 'idle talk' or 'quackery.' This latter category, we suggest, may be even more dangerous, for, as we see it, it is being dismissed as unworthy of defense. We suggest that more attention be paid to the irrational, to the 'characters,' particularly when the example is so striking as in the case described...."

It should be added that the Secret Service has no control over sentences imposed by judges in the Federal courts.

There is an epilogue to this case. Five years after his arrest, Manuel joined the U. S. Marine Corps. One year later he went AWOL (absent without official leave) and was declared a deserter. At the time this book was published, his whereabouts was unknown.

Sadly enough, many threatening letters are from people who are mentally ill. In numerous instances the writers of such letters are sent to state hospitals for treatment, rather than to prison.

As an example, here's a true story about a man who wrote a threatening letter to the President. We'll call him Stanley, but that's not his real name.

Stanley lived in a small Ohio town where he worked as a carpenter. He believed that only he could make the President stop wars and riots, eliminate poverty, and solve all other problems in the world. In his

Anonymous letters on file often ultimately lead to identification of the authors through handwriting characteristics, misspellings, and verbal peculiarities.

letter he wrote, "If you force me, I will go to the people and there will be total hell break loose. I will hang your hide up to dry with the press of my finger, and either you will start to act like a grownup man or it is your funeral."

Stanley believed that Jesus Christ was an impostor and that God was Stanley's right-hand man. Thus Stanley felt he had the power to do anything.

Secret Service agents arrested Stanley for threatening the life of the President. Newspaper reporters were present when he was arraigned, but the agents pointed out that Stanley was undoubtedly mentally ill, and the reporters agreed not to print a story about him at that time.

In Stanley's home the agents found a rifle with a telescopic sight and a .22-caliber pellet-gun.

In court, Stanley made a loud speech proclaiming himself to be "Supreme Protector of the Laws of the World."

An understanding judge suggested that if arrangements could be made to commit Stanley to a hospital, the criminal charges against him might be dismissed. Stanley's family refused to have him sent to a mental hospital, however, evidently because they thought him to be "harmless," and also because of the embarrassment they would feel in admitting that one of their family members might be mentally unsound.

The Federal judge then issued a warrant for Stanley's arrest on the criminal charge of threatening the President. The judge told the Secret Service agents, "I hope that this man's family will prefer to have him treated in a hospital rather than prosecuted as a criminal in this court."

When the agents explained the choice, the family agreed to have Stanley hospitalized. Psychiatrists who examined him reported that he had "schizophrenic reactions, paranoid type." (A schizophrenic retreats from reality, has unpredictable moods, and lives in a world of fantasy. A paranoiac has marked delusions of persecution or of grandeur.)

After two months of psychiatric treatment, Stanley's condition had improved to the point where he was allowed to spend weekends with his family. After six additional months, Stanley's son reported that Stanley had made a remarkable improvement and that his relationship with the family was better than it had been in a long time. Ultimately, Stanley was discharged from the hospital with the understanding that he would visit the outpatient clinic once a month for checkups.

In this case, as in some others, action by the Secret Service brought about a notable improvement in the health of a mentally ill man who might otherwise have come to a tragic end.

Some psychiatrists believe that no person who is mentally unsound should be considered "harmless." Depending upon the type of affliction, in fact, many such people are definitely dangerous to themselves and to others.

Take the case of Martin X, a former American soldier. He was obsessed with the idea that he had wrongfully been given a general discharge for medical reasons. He insisted that he be given a 100-per-cent veteran's disability discharge and allowed to rejoin the army. He also complained that the right side of his face had been crushed while he was boxing for the army, and believed that he had been disfigured. (He hadn't.)

The army granted him several hearings. After one of these he said, "If I don't get more favorable action from the army, I'm going to Washington and kill the whole bunch!"

This was only one of many threats made by Martin. At other times he shouted that he was going to kill a number of officers at West Point.

The climax came when he openly threatened the life of the President. "I'm going up there to Washington and shoot the President in the legs so he can't walk," he said. "I don't want to kill him, I just want to cripple him!"

This threat was reported to the Secret Service in Columbia, South Carolina. Agents there joined deputies from the Greenville County Sheriff's office and set out to arrest Martin X.

First they talked with his mother. Tearfully she agreed that Martin was dangerous. "He has at least two guns," she told the agents, "and I don't think he'll give up without a fight."

Agents and deputy sheriffs talked with some of Martin's friends. One said, "Martin has a small arsenal in his room. He told me that he'd carry a gun wherever he went—just in case."

"Do you think you could induce Martin to leave his home tonight and meet you somewhere?" the agents asked.

The friend nodded slowly. "I think I could. I could ask him to meet me in a hardware store and give me some advice on a few tools I'm considering buying."

Martin agreed to meet his friend at the hardware store, and agents kept him under observation. Later the pair separated and Martin started home. As he neared the house, the agents and deputies moved in to arrest him.

"We're from the Secret Service," one agent said. "We have a warrant for your arrest, Martin."

For a moment Martin stood still, looking wildly into the faces of the arresting officers. Then he stepped backward and reached toward his right hip. Instantly the agents whipped out their guns. Martin pulled out a revolver and aimed it point-blank at one agent. The agent fired one shot, wounding Martin, but not critically. His gun was seized.

More than forty cartridges were found in Martin's pockets, and three boxes of bullets were found hidden under the hood of his car.

Martin's history showed that he had a record of arrests for disorderly conduct, assault and battery, breach of the peace, pointing a pistol at another, and assault with a deadly weapon.

He was soon committed to a hospital to receive treatment for his mental illness.

Some people who threaten the life of the President in writing fail to sign their letters in the belief that their identities will remain secret. They're often mistaken. The Secret Service tracks down many such people in various ways.

In certain instances men and women write *and sign* angry letters to the President or Vice-President, complaining about crime, taxes, poverty, violence, the rising cost of living, housing, and other problems that confront all of us. No government agency or official objects to letters reflecting public opinion, but when these letters contain veiled threats against the President, such as "You ought to be strung up or shot," or "It's time something fatal happened to you," they are referred to the Secret Service.

The Intelligence Division, part of the Office of Protective Intelligence, analyzes and classifies such letters in a number of ways. It has an extensive file of typewriter specimens that enable agents to determine the make of typewriter on which a letter was written.

It has an alphabetical file in which the signed names of the writers are placed.

There is a unique system of handwriting classification in which special codes identify writers' quirks and idiosyncrasies, such as backhand writing, handprinting, peculiar or unusual styles of capital letters, use of punctuation or lack of it, and so on.

Part of the file relates to frequent misspellings of certain words.

Another classifies key words and phrases. One writer, for example, used the expression "gonna" instead of "going to" in several of his letters. Another wrote, "Let me tell you" at the beginning of almost every paragraph.

In many of these cases the letter-writers may gradually become so obsessed and disturbed that they finally decide to threaten to kill the President if he fails to accede to their demands. When they reach that point, however, they usually decide not to sign their names to such threats. Their letters are referred to the Secret Service, where a search of typewriter specimens, or handwriting classifications, or key words or phrases, or misspellings, or other file clues lead to early letters bearing the names and addresses of the writers.

Sometimes another kind of good detective work exposes a culprit. In one instance a typewritten letter indicated that unless the President resigned immediately, the writer would kidnap a member of the President's family.

The stationery used for the letter had evidently borne a printed letterhead that had been cut off. The paper was found to have an unusual watermark design that was not included in the Secret Service file on watermarks. The typewriter specimen file revealed that the writer had used a Royal standard typewriter. Agents visited several paper manufacturers and learned that one had produced this particular paper for only one customer—a major steamship line.

At the steamship offices, agents talked with the general manager and obtained a company letterhead that matched the paper under investigation. They also were given permission to return after closing hours to obtain type specimens from the numerous typewriters in daily use. After nearly two hours, the agents located a Royal whose type matched that on the threatening letter.

The machine was in the small office of a middle-aged man employed as an accounting clerk, and was used by him almost exclusively. The manager told agents that the man had been noticeably disturbed by results of the recent Presidential election and had not hesitated to express the opinion that voters had made a bad choice.

The next morning the agents confronted the clerk, who at first denied authorship of the letter. When he was shown distinctive characteristics of the type impressions as proof that his typewriter was the machine used, he broke down and cried, insisting that he would never have carried out the threat.

He pleaded guilty and was sentenced to serve a year and a day in a Federal penitentiary.

The Secret Service believes that no threat or report of a threat against the President or other officials it protects can be considered lightly, and its agents are constantly making investigations of this kind. In a single year, for instance, the Secret Service received about fifteen thousand "threat-related" cases for investigation. In the same year its agents arrested 338 people for making threats and were involved in 302 convictions or commitments to mental hospitals.

It's important for all of us to remember that every citizen is free to express his opinion to the President or Vice-President on any subject whatever, so long as he or she does not threaten the official or members of his family with bodily harm or death.

If and when such threats are made by writers who cannot be identified by the Protective Intelligence Division, it's possible that leads can be provided by specialists in the Secret Service crime laboratory.

Preparing an exhibit for presentation in Federal Court.

Chapter 15

THE NINHYDRIN TRAP

The Secret Service laboratory specializes in techniques that are useful in its task of protecting the currency and other obligations of the United States. Its specialists make microscopic examinations and comparisons of paper, ink and other features of counterfeit paper money. Ultraviolet and infrared light often contribute useful information to such examinations. Expert photographers and technicians make photographic enlargements of money, checks and handwriting for investigative purposes and also for use as exhibits in court.

But one of the most effective aids in solving crime is the telltale human fingerprint, and fingerprints are of major importance in the specialized work of the Secret Service.

The skin on the tips of your fingers has tiny ridges that are different from the ridges on the fingers of every other person in the world. They do not change from the time you're born until you die.

When persons are arrested and charged with having committed crimes, a special kind of black ink is applied to the first joints of their fingers by police. Each finger and thumb is then rolled from one side of the fingernail to the other on a card, leaving an inked fingerprint impression. The fingers are rolled so that the prints will reveal all of the ridge patterns, which end at the sides of the fingers.

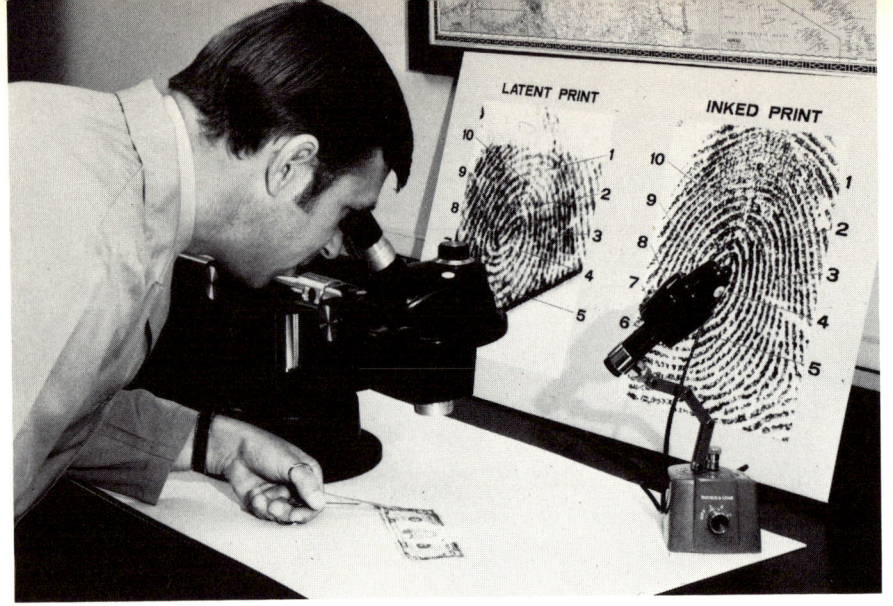

An identification specialist examines a latent fingerprint on a counterfeit note.

These cards are sent to the Federal Bureau of Investigation in Washington, where millions of similar cards are on file. The FBI has a system that sorts the fingerprints into patterns, or types, each with various subdivisions. When new cards come in, the fingerprints are classified, or arranged in groups, according to the ridge patterns. Through this system the fingerprints on a new card can be matched quickly with those recorded on an old card in the file. For example, if a man were arrested and fingerprinted in 1972 and had also been fingerprinted for a different offense in 1965, both sets of his prints would be brought together in this scientific filing system.

One unusual Secret Service case shows how important a fingerprint can be.

The case involved eight men and a seventeen-year-old girl in and around Washington, D. C. It was masterminded by a known gambler and suspected narcotics dealer we'll call Trace. Trace conspired with a Post Office worker to steal a quantity of Federal pension checks from the mails. The checks were dated and due to be delivered on August 1, but the postal employee grabbed a bundle of the checks on July 30. He put them in the bottom of his laundry bag and covered them with dirty clothes that he was permitted to take home for cleaning. The unsuspecting Post Office guards looked at the clothing on top and let the thief pass with the bag.

At home he counted his haul. There were one thousand checks in the bundle, ranging in payable amounts from $200 to $700 each. In all, they totaled about $250,000.

He brought the checks to Trace, who had agreed to pay him one dollar for every stolen check. They met in a motel room. The thief grinned as he held out the bundle of checks. "Here they are, man!" he said. "One thousand checks. You owe me one thousand bucks. Count 'em, if you want."

Trace opened an empty suitcase. "Put 'em in there," he said. "If it's a short count, you'll hear from me." He took a roll of bills from his pocket, counted out a thousand dollars and handed the money to the thief, who departed.

Trace set the rest of his plan in motion. He brought in six of his men friends and his teen-age girl friend, Liz. One of the men, Ziggy (not his real name), was employed as a clerk in a city sanitation department. Trace ordered Ziggy to obtain a blank Sanitation Department identification card of the kind used by city employees. Ziggy stole the card. Trace took it to an underground printer who used it as a model to make a thousand counterfeit cards. These would be used as identification in cashing the stolen checks.

Trace and the others met in his motel room. He opened the suitcase, took out the bundle of checks in one hand, and waved it at the group. "We got a thousand checks for you to cash," he said. He put the bundle back in the suitcase. "But first you gotta sign these cards, to use if you're asked for identification. Ziggy has put the names on the cards with a typewriter. You sign the cards in those names, and then you make sure you sign the backs of the checks with the same names, in the same handwriting."

The group began the forgeries. "Ain't you doin' none, Trace?" one asked.

Trace smiled and shook his head. "I got the checks. I laid out my own dough. Ain't that enough?"

"Sure. I was just askin'."

Many of the checks were supposed to be forwarded to retired people in Florida and other places in the South. These checks were sorted out and burned. The others were addressed to people in Virginia, Maryland and Pennsylvania.

The forgers worked during daily lunch hours and after their regular jobs at night. On August 2 they met and separated into groups. All checks payable to women were given to Liz to cash. The others were divided among the six men.

They rented cars and went to a few Virginia banks where they cashed some checks without difficulty. One day Liz and one of the men, Joey, entered a bank together. Once inside, they separated and went to different tellers to cash the checks. The tellers brought the checks to the manager for approval, but because the man and woman were strangers and had insufficient identification, the manager refused to cash the checks.

The pair left the bank separately. "That's odd," one of the tellers told the manager. "They came in here together."

The manager ran out of the bank just as Liz and Joey joined up again. They saw him and made a dash for their car. A few moments later they drove away, but not before the manager noted the license number.

The manager called the Secret Service and reported the incident. The Secret Service issued an all-points bulletin for the car and its occupants.

That night the Secret Service was notified that FBI agents had arrested Trace for attempting to sell five hundred stolen government checks to a contact from Philadelphia. The checks were not endorsed, and the FBI could charge Trace with only a misdemeanor, for which he was placed on probation for a year. The FBI did not know of his connection with the other stolen checks, and the Secret Service had no information to connect Trace with them.

Checking the license number provided by the bank manager, Secret Service agents learned that the car had been rented in Maryland. At the rental agency they obtained the name and address given by the man who rented the vehicle. Oddly enough, the man had used his real name and address—and for a very good reason. The only thing he knew how to write was his own name and address!

Agents went to his home and arrested Joey. Joey was identified by another bank teller who had cashed a stolen check for him. Then Joey told agents where they could find Liz, and she was arrested. But she was only seventeen and couldn't be prosecuted as an adult. She was brought into Juvenile Court, convicted and placed on probation.

Meantime, another member of the group tried to cash one of the checks, but he was so nervous that the teller became suspicious. The check was payable to someone we'll call "Charles Maraschino." The teller, a woman, asked the customer to write his name on a separate piece of paper, which he did. She took the paper and the unendorsed check to the manager, saying that she was suspicious. She then returned and asked the man to endorse the check.

However, she held the check face down on the counter with one finger, so he could not see the name on the face of the check. After some hesitation he endorsed it "Charles Machinio." The teller looked at the misspelled name and turned to go back to the manager. The man ran out of the bank, somersaulted over the hood of a parked car, and fled.

Another of the forgers was traced through a rented car and denied having been at the bank where one check was cashed. It developed that he and Liz had gone to the bank's drive-in window and cashed the check. As they started to leave, Liz drove the car into the side of the bank building and they had to call a tow truck to get out. A police officer on the scene gave Liz a ticket for reckless driving. The ticket and the officer's testimony proved that the pair had been at the bank, and Secret Service

Handwriting specimens of a suspect are compared with forged signatures on United States Savings Bonds.

handwriting experts proved that the man had forged endorsements on several of the stolen checks.

A number of the checks were recovered from those arrested, although the swindlers had cashed about $100,000 worth before they were caught.

Gradually the Secret Service investigations led to the arrests of all the forgers except Trace, the ringleader. On the basis of the FBI report of Trace's arrest on a minor charge, the Secret Service questioned his accomplices, but none would admit that Trace was involved. He had not forged or cashed any of the thousand stolen checks.

Now the agents gathered up most of the stolen checks, including those that had been cashed, and sent them to the Secret Service laboratory. They also sent a copy of Trace's fingerprints from a previous arrest.

Could the experts find Trace's fingerprints on any of the stolen checks?

In the Identification Section of the Special Investigations and Security Division, lab technicians could try to develop latent fingerprints on the checks by using powders and chemicals, but decided instead to use the ninhydrin fume hood.

The fume hood tops an oblong glass-front cabinet. The glass front can be raised and lowered to permit access to the interior. Inside the cabinet are lines stretched from one end to the other, like clotheslines. Clinging to the lines are spring-type clothespins, used to hold papers or other materials to be tested.

Testing consists of flooding the closed cabinet with fumes of ninhydrin, a chemical that reacts to amino acids, which are secreted in the pores of human skin. The ninhydrin is combined with acetone or ether, which evaporates quickly, leaving ninhydrin crystals on the fingerprints on the paper or document being tested.

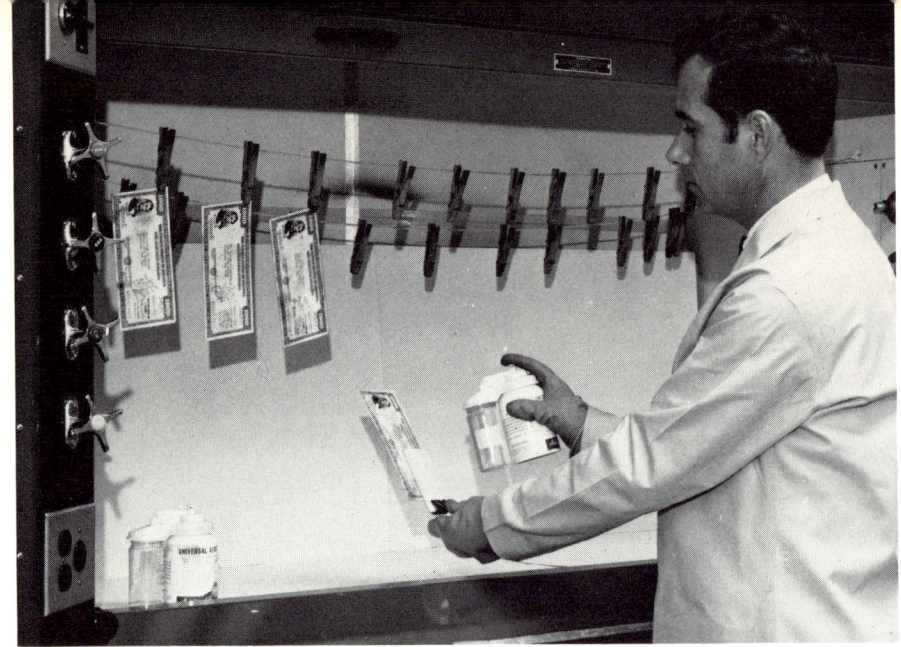

Ninhydrin sprays help develop latent fingerprints.

The examination of the stolen checks for Trace's fingerprints was difficult. The checks had been handled by the forgers and by a number of bank employees, so there were numerous fingerprints or parts of fingerprints on the check faces and backs.

Doggedly, the laboratory experts continued the search, but after comparing fingerprints on several hundred of the checks without finding any made by Trace, they began to be discouraged. Maybe Trace had never handled the checks. Or if he had, perhaps he had worn gloves. Perhaps all the laboratory time and effort was being expended uselessly.

Then, on the morning of the fifth day of the search, one of the fingerprint specialists let out a whoop.

"Bingo!" he cried. "We've made it!"

He had found just one identifiable print of Trace's right thumb. Later, piecing together the whole story, agents deduced that Trace had handled the bundle of checks only once—the night he picked them up and showed them to his accomplices in the motel room. That's when he left the telltale evidence that was destined to send him to prison.

The thumbprint was conclusive proof that Trace had handled the stolen checks. Faced with this fact, some members of his group implicated him in an effort to help themselves. Although Trace had never forged or cashed a single check, he was charged with "aiding and abetting" the forgeries, and with conspiracy. He was convicted and sentenced to serve fifteen years in a Federal penitentiary. Other members of the group were also convicted and sentenced.

History records that more than a thousand years ago the Chinese required every man who signed a legal document to place his thumbprint near his signature. They considered the thumbprint to be a foolproof piece of identification. A thousand years later an American criminal named Trace could testify that the ancient Chinese were clever, indeed.

Chapter 16

MODERN MUSKETEERS

In his fine book, *The Three Musketeers,* Alexander Dumas endowed his heroes with a now-famous slogan—"One for all and all for one!"

This could apply not only to the members and units of the Secret Service itself, but also to some degree to their relationships with other law-enforcement groups.

For instance, local and state police frequently arrest persons for violations of city or state laws, then discover that their prisoners have committed offenses within Secret Service jurisdiction, such as possessing counterfeit money or stolen government checks. And the opposite often happens—Secret Service agents arrest counterfeiters or forgers who are drug pushers or burglars or who have violated local or state laws. In either instance, the enforcement groups exchange information.

Late one night a Secret Service agent walked down a deserted street in a California city when a man suddenly appeared behind him and held a gun against his back.

"This is a stickup!" the man said.

Instantly the agent seized his own revolver, whirled around and grabbed the robber's gun hand. The holdup man, seeing the agent's gun, fell to his knees and folded his hands in supplication.

"Don't shoot, mister!" he begged. "Please don't shoot!"

The agent took him to the nearest police station.

Local and state police play important cooperating roles with the Secret Service whenever the President, the Vice-President, or other dignitary visits various cities. Police officials assign officers to man posts of duty, or to line parade routes, or to help the Secret Service in other ways.

September 23, 1919. President Woodrow Wilson visits Salt Lake City, Utah.

The Secret Service may also work closely with another Treasury enforcement agency, the Alcohol Tax, Tobacco and Firearms Division of the Internal Revenue Service. Among other duties, the ATTFD assigns its agents to crack down on illicit stills—places where people make their own whiskey or corn liquor—prevalent in mountain areas of some Southern states.

The unlawful operators sell their alcoholic products without paying the Government taxes that are paid by lawful distillers. Sometimes they make counterfeit tax stamps to put on their bottles. Under the law, the genuine Government tax stamps are in the same class as currency where counterfeiting is concerned, so the making of bogus stamps is of direct interest to the Secret Service. At the same time, the Secret Service may arrest a currency counterfeiter and find that he is making phony tax stamps, a venture that the ATTFD would be interested in.

There is also close cooperation between the Secret Service and the FBI. The FBI may receive letters threatening the President's life, or may get confidential information about alleged plots to harm or kill the President or Vice-President, or some other official under Secret Service protection. FBI agents may learn about suspected counterfeiters. Any such information is furnished to the Secret Service immediately. And during its criminal investigations, the Secret Service may unearth matters that are normally of interest to the FBI, to which it relays whatever facts are available.

The Secret Service has some of its agents assigned to the Attorney General's Organized Crime Strike Force, where they cooperate with representatives of other Federal agencies in fighting organized crime. In New York City, for example, the Strike Force received information concerning one Charlie Bobo (which isn't his real name), a small-time

An illegal still in a backwoods area is destined for confiscation.

hoodlum who had been convicted of manslaughter and was free on bail, pending appeal.

It was reported that Charlie had sent word to the underworld that he would buy stolen U.S. Savings Bonds—at discounts, of course.

The facts were given to the Secret Service agents on duty with the Strike Force, who began an investigation. From various underworld sources they finally learned that Charlie was enlisting the services of men and women to cash stolen bonds outside New York City. In fact, his accomplices traveled from New York to Florida, cashing bonds along the way, then headed for Arizona, New Mexico and California.

At first, his price for stolen bonds was $7 for $100 in bonds, but as he needed larger quantities, the price climbed to $35 per $100.

Finally, Charlie "discharged" his traveling associates and decided to let his girl friend become his partner. After she cashed about $90,000 in stolen bonds in several places, they took another $60,000 worth to Boston. For identification, the girl obtained a false baptismal certificate which she used to get a United States passport in the name of the bond owner. It worked. She cashed the $60,000 in bonds before she was caught and implicated Charlie.

Charlie never forged or cashed a single bond, but he was convicted and sentenced to serve ten years in prison.

One outstanding example of cooperation took place in October, 1970, during the celebration of the twenty-fifth anniversary of the founding of the United Nations. By direction of the President and the Secretary of the Treasury, the Secret Service was authorized to protect the heads of government, heads of state, and other high-ranking dignitaries who visited the United States to take part in the celebration.

The Secret Service enlisted the help of New York City police, New York State police, the New York Fire Department, representatives of the State and Defense Departments, the FBI, the Customs Bureau, Internal Revenue agents and other Treasury personnel. With this assistance, in a thirty-day period, the Secret Service provided protection for forty-three distinguished visitors from foreign lands.

One other important activity involves Secret Service cooperation with the International Criminal Police Organization, popularly known as Interpol. The Assistant Secretary of the Treasury in charge of Treasury law-enforcement is the official United States representative of Interpol, but he has designated an agent of the Secret Service in Washington as Interpol Bureau Chief.

The prime purpose of Interpol, in its own words, is to "enable police forces in different countries to coordinate their work effectively in the aim of crime prevention and law enforcement." The organization, however, is "forbidden to undertake any activity in connection with cases having political, military, religious or racial character."

On the basis of files relating to more than half a million people, Interpol distributes circulars, "wanted" notices, and information of international interest concerning murder, burglary, car theft, missing persons, bank frauds, smuggling, forgery, drugs, counterfeiting and other crimes.

Counterfeiting information, including descriptions of good and bad money of various nations, is set out in *The Counterfeits and Forgeries Review,* published by Interpol. Copies are sent not only to the Secret Service and other law-enforcement agencies, but also (by subscription) to more than five thousand banks and credit establishments all over the world.

Interpol holds annual international conferences for law-enforcement officials, including periodic conferences dealing exclusively with the crime of counterfeiting as it affects all member countries.

It also makes studies of and reports on all kinds of crime prevention, police department organization, and new techniques of criminal investigation. Many of its findings are circulated in its official publication, *The International Criminal Police Review.*

Interpol's National Central Bureau in the United States is represented by the Secret Service because the Treasury Department has official jurisdiction in the international crimes of counterfeiting and smuggling.

The Secret Service agent at Interpol in Washington can communicate by teletype with forty Interpol members, including Scotland Yard in England, the Italian Questure, the French Surete, Interpol Buenos Aires, Interpol Melbourne (Australia) and the Japanese National Police Agency.

Any police department or other enforcement agency in the United States that needs a criminal investigation or inquiry made in any of the 104 member countries of Interpol may make a request to Interpol in Washington by letter, telephone, telegram, or through the Secret Service by way of the Law Enforcement Telecommunications System (LETS).

LETS is a computerized law-enforcement teletype switching system centered in Phoenix, Arizona. By means of this system the Secret Service, for example, can send or receive messages from nearly five thousand police departments throughout the United States. A typical transmission might look like this:

```
280  DCSS101  U. S.  SECRET SERVICE  WASH  DC
010171   ALL POINTS BULLETIN — NATIONWIDE
FOLLOWING SUBJECT WANTED FOR VIOLATION
TITLE 18 SEC 871 U. S. CODE; WARRANT
OUTSTANDING. ANY INFORMATION ON SUBJECT'S
WHEREABOUTS NOTIFY SECRET SERVICE
WASHINGTON, D. C.   TELEPHONE OR REPLY
VIA L.E.T.S.  DODO,  WILLIE H.  MALE  WHITE
DOB/010337  HT/5-9  WT/180  EYES/BLUE
HAIR/BROWN
SOC SEC NR/594-456-3030
USSS CASE NR/CO-2-463955   FBI NR/326-399C
ALIASES: BRUMMEL, BOBO
         HANSOME, HORATIO
         JACKSON, ANDREW
AUTH SPEC AGT IN CHG
US SECRET SERVICE  WASH DC  REK  1002 EST
```

Another source of instant communication for law-enforcement groups is the National Crime Information Center (NCIC), operated by the FBI. Basically, the NCIC stores important information about crimes and criminals in a centralized computer, with computer terminals at various strategic points. One terminal is in the Secret Service Communications Division in Washington.

Requests for information from the computer can be answered promptly, often an important factor in criminal investigations. For instance, the Secret Service gets serial numbers of stolen savings bonds from the Treasury's Division of Loans and Currency, and feeds these numbers into the NCIC system. One day a New York City bank telephoned the New York Secret Service office, saying that a young couple was in the bank trying to cash $8,500 worth of savings bonds that had

(Left) Computers are an invaluable modern aid in storing and gathering essential information quickly and efficiently. (Above) A communications technician prepares a message entry for storage in the National Crime Information Center (NCIC).

been issued in Colorado. The bank wanted to know whether the Secret Service had any information concerning the bonds.

The New York office telephoned Secret Service headquarters in Washington and supplied the bond serial numbers. A fast check with the NCIC computer showed that all the bonds had been stolen. The New York bank was so informed and asked to detain the young couple. As bank guards approached them, the girl managed to run out of the bank. One guard held the man and the other pursued the girl, catching her on the street just a few yards from the bank entrance.

The man and woman were prosecuted and convicted as bond thieves and forgers. Except for the swift response from NCIC, they might yet be at liberty, still stealing and forging savings bonds.

There is one other important enforcement group with which the Secret Service maintains cordial relations. The International Association of Chiefs of Police (IACP), with headquarters in Washington, has a wide membership of police chiefs and their staffs from numerous cities in the United States, Canada and Mexico. Other members include representatives of various Federal, state and county enforcement groups. The Secret Service Director, his assistant directors, and most special agents in charge of field offices belong to the IACP; they are often invited to take part in its programs and are thus able to discuss mutual enforcement problems with police officials who are, after all, the first line of community defense against crime.

William P. Wood, first Chief of the U.S. Secret Service.

Chapter 17

LEADERS AND LAURELS

The Secret Service is justly proud of its accomplishments and reputation in the field of law enforcement. To a great degree this feeling of pride stems from policies and rules laid down by the men who have been privileged to head the organization since its beginning in 1865.

Now well into its second century, the Secret Service, as of 1971, has been under the direction of only fourteen men.

Its first Chief, William P. Wood, was a fearless swashbuckler who had frequently penetrated Confederate lines during the Civil War to gather invaluable information about troop movements for the Union forces. Wood was no angel, for in his earlier days he had turned a few unscrupulous tricks for pay, but after he was chosen as the first Secret Service leader he dedicated himself to the Number One task, the suppression of counterfeiting, and did it efficiently.

When Wood resigned in 1869 he was succeeded by Herman C. Whitley of Virginia, an Internal Revenue tax assessor. Whitley was recommended for the Chief's job by Major General Benjamin Butler, who had observed Whitley during the Civil War as a Union scout and a bold cavalry leader. Whitley made an imposing appearance. He was nearly seven feet tall and had a black mustache, a small neat beard, and piercing blue eyes.

Whitley dismissed some agents (their title then was "operatives"), set up a new system of criminal records, and ordered all agents to submit written reports describing their activities during each 24-hour period.

Until the time of Whitley's administration, the only credentials an agent carried were in the form of a letter on Treasury Department stationery, identifying him as a "Secret Service Operative." In many instances an agent, approaching people to get information in criminal cases, found that it was looked upon with some suspicion. Chief Whitley decided to equip each agent with an official badge and more impressive printed credentials.

Many badge designs were considered and one was finally chosen on August 5, 1873. It was the five-pointed silver star mentioned in an earlier chapter. When the badges were issued, each agent received a notice from Whitley to the effect that "the cost price, $25, should be deposited by each officer (which amount will be deducted from your account for the current month), to be returned upon your retirement from the Service."

Final versions of the printed credentials—the commissions—were produced in the Bureau of Engraving and Printing and issued to all agents on March 17, 1875 (after Whitley's resignation).

Because most of the counterfeiting, forgery and other criminal activity centered in and around New York City, Whitley asked that Secret Service headquarters be moved to that city. Permission was granted, and the Chief opened his office at 63 Bleecker Street, although a small clerical force remained on duty in Washington. A selection of important criminal files accompanied Whitley to New York in a "small black leather-covered trunk."

It was during Whitley's administration that the Secret Service was directed to investigate actions of the growing Ku Klux Klan (Chapter 3).

In 1871, Washington was rocked by a scandal involving questionable activities of the District of Columbia government. During an investigation Whitley's name was mentioned, with an implication that he had been a conspirator. There was no proof, but the Chief's reputation had been tainted and the Secretary of the Treasury asked Whitley to resign, which he did on September 2, 1874.

A month later, on October 2, 1874, Elmer Washburn replaced Whitley as Secret Service Chief. Washburn was Chief of Police in Chicago and had also been Warden of Joliet Penitentiary. He had thick brown hair, long sideburns that joined with a rather bushy mustache, and walked ramrod-straight.

The headquarters office in New York was closed and returned to the fourth floor of the Treasury Building in Washington, where the entire office staff consisted of three young male clerks and a girl who duplicated letters on a copy-press. One of Washburn's innovations was a new device,

Chiefs of the U.S. Secret Service.

a Sholes-Glidden-Remington typewriter, which the girl was trained to use to replace the copy-press.

Elmer Washburn remained in office only two years, resigning voluntarily to go into private business. His successor, James J. Brooks, was the first Chief to be promoted from the ranks of Treasury investigators.

Brooks had an interesting background. Born in Birmingham, England, he had come to the United States in 1848 at the age of twenty-four. After the California gold rush of '49, there was a great push westward. In 1851, Brooks became the leader of a pioneer group bound for Minnesota Territory, and after rugged weeks of travel by rail, boat, covered wagon and on foot, he brought his band safely to Reed's Landing. The group included his wife and two children. The Brooks family stayed in Minnesota for three years, then made their way to New York and sailed for England, but only for a short visit. They returned to live in Newark, New Jersey, later moving to Washington, D.C., where Brooks earned a reputation as a crusading crime reporter for the Washington *Chronicle*.

His renown precipitated an offer to become an Internal Revenue agent, which he accepted. He proved to be a fearless one-man enforcement army, nailing big-time tax evaders and exposing high-level corruption in almost all states.

So effective was his work that Brooks found himself the target of an underworld "contract." Unknown sources offered $500 to anyone who would murder him. Two thugs tried. One hit him with a blackjack. The other shot him. Both men were caught and punished, and although Brooks lived, the bullet that lodged in his chest remained there for years.

When Elmer Washburn resigned, Brooks became his successor.

Brooks had one major difficulty that plagued the Secret Service for many years. He could not persuade Congress to appropriate money for new agents or for equipment needed to permit the Service to operate at peak efficiency. His budgets were cut severely—in one instance a request for $11,500 (the amount allowed his predecessor the year before) was slashed to $3,500. To do the best with what he had, Brooks ruled that no agents could take vacations and that any leaves of absence would be without pay.

In 1885, Brooks tried to resign, but the Secretary of the Treasury pleaded with him to stay, and he agreed. He tried once again in 1889, and although he did resign as Chief, he was persuaded by the Secretary of the Treasury to conduct certain important investigations as a "special agent." Brooks finally retired on February 16, 1893.

His successor to the Chiefship in 1889 was John S. Bell, who had joined the Secret Service as an operative on June 22, 1885, after he had established an enviable reputation in law enforcement as Chief of Police in Newark, New Jersey.

Bell was a husky six-footer who wore ten-gallon cowboy hats. With his gray mustache, long hair and a rather bushy goatee, he could double for William "Buffalo Bill" Cody. He was an expert pistol shot, fast on the draw, and an excellent horseman.

Bell ran into some of the financial obstacles faced by those before him—insufficient money for needed manpower and equipment. Counterfeiting was on a decided upswing, and bankers and other victims of counterfeiters and forgers were clamoring for Secret Service action. Chief Bell asked the Secretary of the Treasury to plead with Congress for more funds, but the Secretary refused, largely because the Government was then involved in an economy wave to lower costs.

Bell kept insisting on the need for more funds. Finally, the Secretary sent him a one-line memorandum dated June 2, 1890. It read: "Your services as Chief of the Secret Service will not be required on and after this date."

No immediate successor was at hand, and for some seven months the Service was under the direction of its Chief Clerk, John Cowie, as Acting Chief. Not until January 2, 1891, was a new leader appointed. He was Andrew L. Drummond, a twenty-year Secret Service veteran.

Drummond had operated a private detective agency in New York City for several years and had accepted an appointment to the Secret Service in 1871. He had risen to the rank of Agent in Charge of the New York District by the time he was chosen to direct the activities of the organization.

Chief Drummond was concerned about a number of legal loopholes in Federal laws that hindered the prosecution of counterfeiters. He worked constantly to plug these loopholes and managed to have fourteen of them eliminated by Congressional amendments during his administration.

On January 31, 1894, Drummond elected to resign to return to his private detective agency with his son as a partner.

With the Chief's position now open, the Secretary of the Treasury was flooded with letters from friends, from Senators and Congressmen and other politicians, all recommending names to be considered for appointment as Secret Service Chief.

Secretary John G. Carlisle decided to ignore them all and to promote directly from Secret Service ranks. His choice was Agent William P. Hazen of the Cincinnati, Ohio, District. Young Hazen had done extensive detective work for his father, Lawrence, who ran the Hazen Detective Agency in Cincinnati for many years. His promotion was certainly one of the fastest on record. He entered the Secret Service as an agent on May 26, 1893. Some nine months later, February 1, 1894, he was appointed Chief.

At that time, the entire country was in the grip of a depression, following the financial panic of 1893. Unemployment was rampant and spreading, and cities and towns were seething with discontent. In Ohio, a forty-year-old small-time politician, Jacob Selcher ("General") Coxey, began to recruit an "army" of unemployed men for a march on Washington. Coxey's aim was to compel Congress to authorize the spending of $500,000,000 to improve streets and public works, thus providing work and pay for thousands of jobless men.

Chief Hazen sent two undercover agents to join Coxey's army. The agents, J. W. Cribbs and Schuyler A. Donnella, trudged to Washington with some six hundred "hard-looking vagabonds, footsore and weary," reporting to Hazen as they went. On May 1, Coxey and his followers assembled on the Capitol grounds in Washington to demonstrate. Many were promptly arrested, along with "General" Coxey, who was held in jail until June 10, and then released. (Coxey later served as Mayor of Massillon, Ohio, from 1931 to 1933.)

In 1898, a wave of counterfeit $100 bills swept through the Eastern states. So deceptive were the counterfeits that Chief Hazen notified banks that the bills would "warrant the recall of all notes of this kind from circulation."

Lyman Gage, Secretary of the Treasury, ordered Hazen to take every action to track down the counterfeiters, even to the point of having Hazen do some of the investigative legwork himself. It appears that during this period Chief Hazen assigned two or three agents to provide security for the President of the United States and his family while they vacationed at Gray Gables, Massachusetts. There was no authority for such action, and newspaper editorials became sharply critical of the Chief, insisting that Federal funds for the Secret Service were to be spent only for the suppression of counterfeiting.

Secretary Gage assigned a Treasury personnel officer to take over Secret Service administrative duties, and demoted Hazen to the rank of agent, a post which he held until he resigned on June 12, 1901.

Now the Secret Service came under the direction of a bold, intelligent and progressive criminologist named John E. Wilkie. A former ace crime reporter, foreign correspondent, and editor of the Chicago *Tribune,* John Wilkie used nerve, logic and brilliant deductions to bring to justice numerous killers, thieves and other criminals who had long outwitted Chicago police.

Wilkie became Secret Service Chief on February 28, 1898.

Immediately he concentrated efforts to trace the source of the deceptive counterfeit $100 bills. He led a small squad of picked agents to check leads in New York and Philadelphia. The Philadelphia leads

A stroll in the park by President William Howard Taft—with Secret Service men.

revealed the names of two likely suspects—Arthur Taylor and Baldwin S. Bredell—who owned an engraving shop.

Taylor and Bredell were kept under surveillance and were observed visiting a tobacco warehouse. Wilkie and his agents obtained a search warrant and late one night entered the warehouse secretly. In it they found the entire manufacturing plant and the engraved plates for the bogus $100 bills.

Next day the agents waited outside until Taylor, Bredell and two accomplices entered the warehouse to work on the press. Then Wilkie and his men rushed in and placed all four under arrest. All were convicted and sentenced to serve twelve years in a Federal prison.

It was under Wilkie's supervision that agents smashed a ring of Spanish spies during the Spanish-American War (Chapter 3). He also broke up the crooked Louisiana Lottery and the monopoly of meat packers popularly known as the "Beef Trust." During Wilkie's fourteen years as Chief he advanced the Secret Service into one of the nation's most fearless and most efficient law-enforcement bodies. He elected to leave the Service in 1912 to accept the presidency of a giant public utilities company in Chicago, where he served ably for many years.

Wilkie made his own recommendation for his successor and it was accepted. The new Chief was William J. Flynn, Agent in Charge of the New York District of the Secret Service. He was sworn in as Chief on December 18, 1912.

Flynn had been Chief of Detectives in the New York Police Department before he became a Secret Service agent. He had been in the Service for fifteen years by the time he was appointed to lead it.

Flynn accepted the appointment on condition that he could live in his native New York City, although the Secret Service administrative headquarters remained in Washington.

Flynn was a popular Chief who frequently accompanied his agents on raids or on investigative assignments. He was instrumental in breaking up the Mafia "Black Handers" and in helping to expose the German sabotage plot involving Dr. Heinrich Albert (Chapter 3).

During World War I, President Woodrow Wilson established the U.S. Food Administration to prevent food monopolies and hoarding. As its head he appointed Herbert Hoover, who promptly asked that the Secret Service be authorized to make necessary investigations for the agency, and this authority was granted.

Flynn's agents also investigated irregularities in the Federal Farm Loan System, exposed numerous people and firms who were trading with the enemy, and also arrested a few thousand counterfeiters and check forgers.

Chief Flynn elected to resign in order to head the Flynn Detective Agency in New York, a successful venture in which he was joined by his sons.

September, 1919. President Woodrow Wilson doffs his hat to San Franciscans.

The next Chief was William Herman Moran, appointed January 2, 1918. Moran began his Secret Service career as an eighteen-year-old messenger for Chief Brooks in 1882. After he won a promotion to Clerk, he began to study case histories of criminals, methods used by counterfeiters and forgers, and techniques of engraving. He also often accompanied agents on investigations at night to become familiar with field work.

In 1897 he became Chief Clerk, and in 1907, he was appointed Assistant Chief of the Secret Service.

Moran's Secret Service career spanned fifty-five years, nineteen as Chief. Under his able direction, agents investigated the Teapot Dome oil scandals, unearthed numerous violations of the 1934 Gold Reserve Act involving the hoarding or unlawful possession of gold coin and gold bullion, broke up scores of major counterfeiting plants, and developed various new security techniques for the protection of the President and members of his family.

Chief Moran also faced the old problem of lack of money for the Service. As late as the 1930's there were counterfeiting cases in which funds were needed by undercover agents to buy bogus bills to be used later as evidence. In many such cases the genuine money was provided by all agents in a field office, who pooled their personal funds and hoped the cash would be recovered when the case was completed.

April, 1921. President Warren G. Harding arrives in New York City.

Buying new office equipment was often out of the question, and the Secret Service was made to take what equipment it needed from "surplus property" discarded by other government agencies.

Chief Moran did everything he could to operate effectively. He came to know virtually every agent and every clerk in the Service by his first name, and was always available and willing to listen to their suggestions and problems, official or personal.

When Chief Moran retired in 1937 at the age of 72 (he had been asked twice by President Franklin D. Roosevelt to stay past the compulsory retirement age of 70), he received the then prevailing maximum retirement pension of $1,200 per year. (Secret Service pensions are now exceptionally generous.) Beloved by his agents throughout the Service, the Chief was happily surprised when many agents and clerks from field offices all over the country met in Washington at a banquet with the Chief as guest of honor. He was presented with letters of good wishes and appreciation from every employee in the Service, and also with the keys to a brand-new automobile bought with money they had all contributed.

Secretary of the Treasury Henry Morgenthau appointed Frank J. Wilson, an Agent in Charge of the Intelligence Division of the Internal Revenue Service, as Moran's successor. In law-enforcement circles Frank Wilson was credited with two major accomplishments. As an Internal Revenue agent he had insisted that the serial numbers of the ransom bills paid to the kidnapper of Charles Lindbergh's son be recorded before the bills were released. Later, a car license number written on one of the ransom bills led to the arrest and ultimate conviction and execution of Bruno Richard Hauptmann for the kidnapping and murder of the baby.

The other victory was the arrest and conviction of Chicago underworld czar Al Capone. For years, attempts to implicate Capone in a multitude of rackets and underworld killings failed for lack of evidence. He was finally found guilty of income-tax evasion on the basis of evidence unearthed and developed by Frank Wilson while the latter was still in Internal Revenue.

Among other innovations, Chief Wilson launched an intense "Know Your Money" program, designed to show storekeepers and others how to detect counterfeit bills and coins and thus avoid losses. With the help of private industry, the Secret Service blanketed the nation with "Know Your Money" booklets, pamphlets, posters, educational movies and other materials aimed at defeating the counterfeiter. The successful passing of bogus bills and coins became less frequent, and agents continued to capture operational plants turning out great quantities of counterfeit money.

During World War II, Chief Wilson's agents had the responsibility for safeguarding not only the President and members of his family, but also Princess Martha of Norway, Queen Wilhelmina of The Netherlands,

President and Mrs. Franklin D. Roosevelt lead the 1941 inaugural motorcade along Pennsylvania Avenue, flanked by Secret Service security.

and other distinguished persons from abroad who were temporarily living in the United States.

Frank Wilson served as Chief until April 30, 1946, when he was promoted to Chief Coordinator of all Treasury Enforcement Agencies. He left that post in December, 1946, to accept the presidency of the National Association of Retired Civil Employees in Washington.

The next Secret Service leader was James J. Maloney, who had served as Wilson's Assistant Chief since 1943. Maloney had spent several years as a patrolman and detective in the Binghamton (N.Y.) Police Department, and as a New York State trooper before being appointed as a Secret Service agent on March 9, 1931.

Subsequently he was placed in charge of various field offices, including the one in New York City, from which he went to Washington as Assistant Chief.

As Chief, Maloney faced one of the old, old troubles—slashes in the Secret Service budget. In 1947, for lack of funds, he was forced to release 63 agents, 22 clerks, 29 White House Police officers and 63 uniformed Treasury guards.

Counterfeiting began to increase, partly because criminals in Europe were making bogus American currency and smuggling it into the United States. Chief Maloney assigned an experienced agent, Guy H. Spaman, to establish an office in Paris and work with foreign police. Spaman assisted authorities in France, England, Italy and many other European countries to track down and arrest scores of manufacturers and distributors of counterfeit American money. By 1951 this onslaught was so successful that Spaman was returned to the United States and appointed Agent in Charge of the Los Angeles Secret Service District.

In 1948 Chief Maloney was promoted by Secretary John Snyder to serve as Chief Coordinator of the Treasury Enforcement Agencies, and U. E. Baughman, Special Agent in Charge of the New York District, was chosen to succeed him as Chief.

Baughman, who had joined the Secret Service as a clerk in Philadelphia, had served as an agent for several years before accepting the top spot in the New York District. After twenty-one years in the Service he was selected as its new Chief on November 29, 1948.

One of his first important official accomplishments was the preparation and distribution of a new comprehensive Manual of Instructions. Until that time, Secret Service instructions had been issued in the form of circular letters, as occasion demanded. Chief Baughman's new manual provided every agent and every clerk with detailed instructions for conducting every kind of Secret Service investigation and for the preparation and submission of every type of official report and form.

He also set up, for the first time, a system whereby each field office would be inspected frequently by qualified headquarters personnel.

Chief Baughman organized a new Management Committee to study suggestions from the field, to make a continuing review of Service actions and policies, and to confer with him biweekly as to their findings and proposals.

One of the most important advances in Secret Service history took place at Chief Baughman's instigation. Since its very beginning, the Secret Service had drawn its authority from annual Congressional appropriation acts; that is, its very existence depended upon a yearly appropriation of money by Congress.

In order to give the Service solid and permanent authority and identity, Chief Baughman sponsored the drafting of a new law defining Secret Service duties in detail. The law was passed by Congress and approved by President Truman on July 16, 1951. It was later amended to add new security duties (see Chapter 10).

When Chief Baughman decided to retire in 1961, he ended a Secret Service career of some thirty-four years, thirteen as head of the organization.

His successor represented another promotion from the ranks. James J. Rowley entered the Secret Service as a special agent in 1938 in New York City, where he was born. After graduating with a master's degree in law from St. John's University in Brooklyn, he became an

James J. Rowley, Director, United States Secret Service.

Agents keep a watchful eye on crowds during the 1969 Inaugural Parade.

investigator for the New York State Banking Department, and later a special agent in the FBI.

In 1939 Rowley was transferred to the Presidential Protective Division (then known as the White House Detail), and was named its Special Agent in Charge in 1947, a post he held until he was appointed Director of the Secret Service on September 1, 1961.

During his career he has served six Presidents—Franklin D. Roosevelt, Harry S. Truman, Dwight D. Eisenhower, John F. Kennedy, Lyndon B. Johnson and Richard M. Nixon. His duties have taken him to all parts of the world. He has received numerous awards, including the Treasury's Exceptional Civilian Service Medal and the President's Award for Distinguished Federal Civilian Service. In 1963 he was chosen by the National Civil Service League as an outstanding Federal career employee.

Director Rowley, who has always shown special interest in the activities and welfare of young people, was presented with the "Mr. Sam

Award" by the Touchdown Club of Washington. This honor, named for the late Sam Rayburn, Speaker of the House of Representatives, is given annually to a Government figure who has fostered and contributed to the progress of sports.

Rowley has also continued a tradition begun by Chief Frank Wilson —the enrollment of Honorary Junior Members of the Secret Service. Youngsters chosen for this honor get handsome certificates of membership signed by the Director and the appropriate Special Agent in Charge. Each certificate sets out these "Principles of Membership":

> "I will help the Secret Service by
> Upholding and defending the Constitution and obeying the laws of the United States,
> Respecting the rights and property of others,
> Obeying my parents, faithfully attending school, and doing all in my power to be a good citizen,
> Showing my respect for the police officers who protect my community."

Director Rowley's responsibilities are heavier than those of most of his predecessors, because he has to oversee activities of the new Executive Protective Service, the Foreign Dignitary Protective Division, and a force of Secret Service agents larger in number and more extensive in duties than any since 1865. His own field experience in counterfeiting and forgery investigations, and his extensive duty with the Presidents, covering most of the world, stand him in good stead as the Secret Service leader.

One of his hoped-for aims is greater public support of law enforcement. "The war on crime and civil disorder," he said, "will not abate as long as citizens refuse to support their police. Some citizens do little to concern themselves with crime and disorder unless it affects them personally. Such lack of public support was and is a vital factor in shaping the problems that confront us today. Public inaction helps crime and civil disorder to flourish. Citizen inactivity gives confidence to those who wish to depreciate our society."

Like the leaders and agents before him, Director Rowley takes intense pride in Secret Service achievements and traditions.

For more impartial views, I asked a few important people if they would care to express an opinion about the Secret Service, based upon their personal experiences and observations.

President Richard M. Nixon replied, "For the past eighteen years, I have frequently had at my side one or more quiet young men with an air of vigilance and strength about them. They have been agents of the U.S. Secret Service, responsible for the protection of the President, the Vice-President, Presidential candidates, and their families. These men

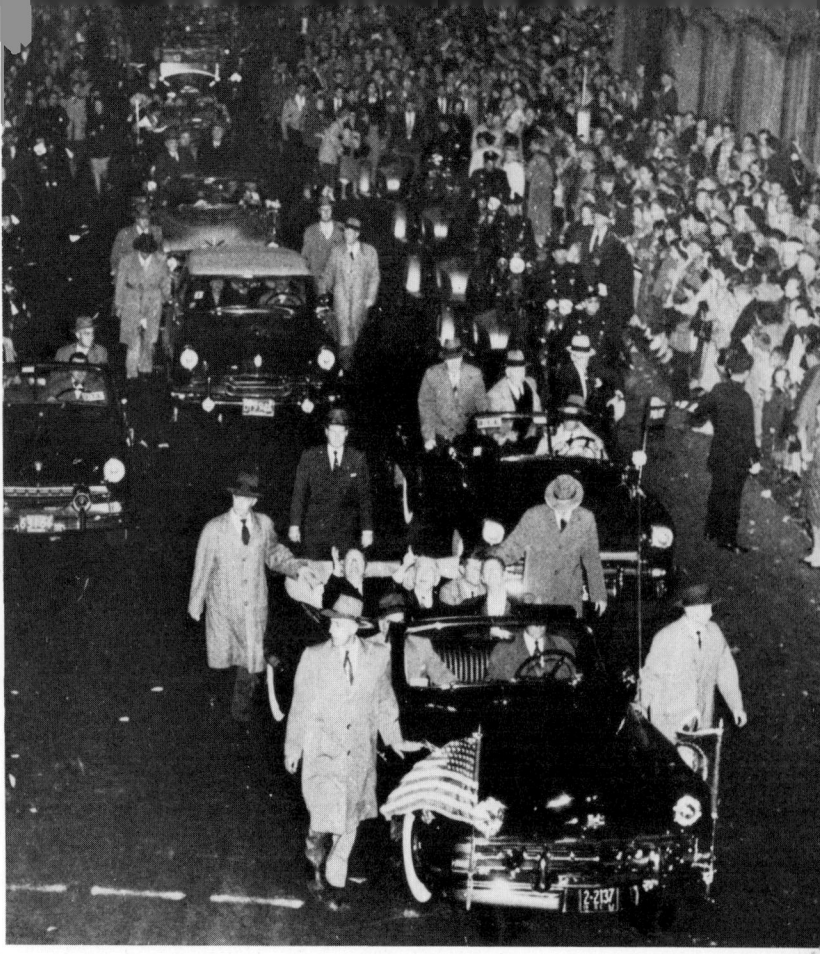

(Above) Agents on assignment with the President dress according to the occasion. At Mr. Nixon's left is Robert Taylor, in charge of the Presidential Protective Division. (Right) President Harry S. Truman (standing) rides through Boston streets in 1952. In the same car is the later President, John F. Kennedy.

have earned my lasting admiration for the selflessness, courage, and superb professionalism with which they do their jobs. It is a high public trust: that neither accident nor malice be permitted to deprive the people of their elected leaders. The Secret Service excels in it. I count it a great privilege to have witnessed the magnificent teamwork of the Secret Service and to have been associated with the able and dedicated men who are its agents."

Former President Harry S. Truman answered, "The Presidency, because of its nature, is a very lonely existence for the occupant. The Secret Service was to me not only a source of constant vigilance but, in a personal way, a source of comfort. In my walks I felt that I was provided with a combination of the highest professional security and ofttimes with intelligent companionship."

Former President Lyndon B. Johnson has paid many tributes to the Secret Service. While still in the White House, in presenting a special award to Director Rowley, the President told him, "...of all the employees that I have known in the Federal government in the thirty-eight years that I have worked, from doorkeeper to secretary, to Congressman, Senator, and Vice-President, I don't believe that I have ever seen any collective group that is possessed with as much integrity, as much character, as much selflessness, and as much courage as your men."

Mr. Johnson also said, "You hear a lot about the FBI. I admire them and applaud them. But I don't yield to them a bit in integrity and competency when you talk about the Secret Service."

Former Vice-President Hubert H. Humphrey said, "I have never known men of more outstanding character and integrity. Daily they impressed me with their amiability, their competence, their devotion to duty. It was not a hindrance, but a tremendous help to have them ever with me during the years that I was Vice-President. I know full well that not one of them would hesitate to give his own life to save the life of the man he was defending. They will always have my admiration and complete devotion."

Mrs. Mamie Doud Eisenhower, widow of the late President, said, "It was a great comfort to General Eisenhower and to me to have the protection of these efficient and loyal agents during the White House years. Now that I am alone it means even more to me to have a feeling of security and to know that I can travel anywhere in safety due to the presence of these gentlemen who are so devoted to their duties."

In its first hundred years, the Secret Service has built up a reputation and tradition unmatched in American law-enforcement circles. Its agents are respected by the police, the courts, the public, even by many of the lawbreakers they have arrested, and by representatives of most of the nations of the world with whom the Secret Service has conducted official business.

Every member of the Secret Service is dedicated to the vital task of protecting the leaders of our country, the currency of our country, and to performing his assigned duties with the integrity and courage that are the watchwords of this famous crime-fighting organization.

Whether special agent, staff member, clerk, technician, Executive Protective Service or Treasury Security Force officer, the men and women of the United States Secret Service are indeed "worthy of trust and confidence."

Dwight D. Eisenhower, as President, prepares to throw the first baseball in an opening game in Washington. Note the Secret Service agents with eyes on the crowd. Presidents-yet-to-be Lyndon B. Johnson and Richard M. Nixon may also be seen in this picture.

INDEX

A

Agents, training of, 59-68
Agnew, Spiro T. (photo), 78
Albert, Dr. Heinrich, 25, 114
Alcohol, Tobacco Tax and Firearms Division, IRS, 64, 102
Alderman, Horace, 60
American Express Company, 68
American Revolution, 29
Assignat, French, 29
Authority, Secret Service, 71-72
Automobiles, Presidential, 74-75

B

Badges, Secret Service, 63, 108
Baker, Lafayette C., 19
Baldinger, Major O. M., 83
Banks, money issued by, 16
Baughman, U. E., 118
"Beef Trust," 113
Bell, John S., 110-111
Birdzell, Donald T., 81-83
Blair House, 71, 81-83
Bobo, Charlie, 102-103
Bomb carrier, Secret Service, 76-77
Bonaparte, Napoleon, 29
Bonds, forged Savings, 55-58, 105-106
Booth, John Wilkes, 18, 69
Boring, Floyd M., 81-82
Boyd, Ben, 21
Bredell, Baldwin S., 113
Brenner, Victor D., 38
Brooks, James J., 110, 115
Brown, Adam, 57-58
Brown, Mary, 57-58
"Bugs," 76-77
Burke, Frank, 25
Burned money, 47-49
Butler, Gen. Benjamin, 107

C

Capone, Al, 116
Carlisle, John G., 111
Carranza, Señor Ramón, 22-23
Castro, Fidel, 89
Cermak, Anton, 70-71
Chase, Salmon P., 45
Checks, Government, forgery of, 50-54, 96-100
Chiefs, Secret Service, 107-120
Chronicle, Washington, 110
Civil War, 17, 107
Cleveland, Grover, 45
Cody, William (Buffalo Bill), 111
Coffelt, Leslie, 81-83
Coins, counterfeit and altered, 37-40
Collazo, Oscar, 81-82
Commission, Secret Service, 63, 108
Connally, John B., Jr., 11, 13
Constitution, U.S., 79
Continental currency, 29
Coolidge, Calvin, 25
Counterfeit money, how to detect, 43-45
Counterfeiting, 27-45
Counterfeits and Forgeries Review, The, 104
"Cowboy," 32-35
Cowie, John, 111
Cox, Edward, 67
Coxey, Jacob Selcher, 112
Craig, William, 60
Cribbs, J. W., 112
Crime laboratory, 94-100
Currency, mutilated, 47-49
Customs, Bureau of, 20, 64, 80, 104
Czolgosz, Leon, 70

D

Daugherty, Harry M., 25
Davidson, Joseph C., 81
DaVinci, Leonardo, 79
Declaration of Independence, 79
Denver Mint, 38
Donnella, Schuyler A., 112
Downs, Joseph H., 82-83
Drug addicts, thefts by, 53
Drummond, Andrew L., 111
Dumas, Alexander, 101

E

Eisenhower, David, 67
Eisenhower, Dwight D., 74, 122
Eisenhower, Mrs. Mamie Doud, 122
English money, counterfeiting of, 29
Engraving and Printing, Bureau of, 45, 108
EPS, 73
Executive Protective Service (EPS), 73, 76-77, 83-86, 120

F

Fall, Albert B., 25
FBI, 24, 78, 80, 96, 98, 102, 104, 119
Federal Reserve Note (diagram), 47
Federal Reserve System, 68
Fingerprints, 95-96
Firearms, use of, 64
Flynn, William J., 113-114
"Follow-up" car, 11
Foreign Dignitary Protective Division, 73
Foreign Missions Division, EPS, 85
Forged bonds, 55-58
Forgery, check, 50-54, 96-100
Forster, 48-49

Fractional currency, 17
Franklin, Benjamin, 45
"Funeral Ben," 56

G

Gage, Lyman, 112
Garfield, James A., 14, 69-70
Government Printing Office, 45
Grant, Ulysses S., 45
Green goods machine, 20
"Greenbacks," 17
Greenbriar, The, 68
Greer, William R., 11
Guiteau, Charles, 69-70
Guns, use of, 64
Gutenberg Bible, 79

H

Hamilton, Alexander, 45
Handwriting classification, 93
Harding, Warren G., 25, 83, 115
Hauptmann, Bruno Richard, 116
Hazen, William P., 111-112
Hill, Clint, 12, 13
Historical documents, safeguarding, 79
Hitler, Adolf, 29
Hoover, Herbert, 83
Hughes, Jack, 21-22
Humphrey, Hubert H., 122

I

IACP, 106
Inspectors, Secret Service, 68
Intelligence Division, IRS, 64
Internal Revenue Service (IRS), 64, 80, 102, 104, 116
International Association of Chiefs of Police (IACP), 106
International Criminal Police Organization (INTERPOL), 104-105
International Criminal Police Review, The, 104
INTERPOL, 104-105

J

Jackson, Andrew, 45, 69
Jefferson, Thomas, 45
"Jim the Penman," 17
Johnson, Lyndon B., 11-14, 74, 121-122
Justice, Department of, 24

K

Kellerman, Roy H., 11, 13
Kennedy, Jacqueline, 11-12
Kennedy, John F., 11-14, 71, 74, 121
Know Your Money, 45, 116
Ku Klux Klan, 22-24, 108

L

Laboratory, crime, 94-100
Land frauds, 24

Law Enforcement Telecommunications System (LETS), 105
LETS, 105
Letters, threatening, 88-94
Lincoln, Abraham, 14, 21-22, 45, 69
Lincoln, Robert, 21
Lincoln's Second Inaugural Address, 79
Lindbergh, Charles, 116
Listening devices, 76-77
Loans and Currency, Division of, 58, 105
Louisiana Lottery, 23, 113

M

Madison, James, 45
Mafia, 23-24, 114
Magna Carta, 79
Maloney, James J., 117-118
"Mammoth Oil Company," 25
Manual, Secret Service, 65, 118
Martha, Princess, 116
Martin X, 92-93
McCulloch, Hugh, 18-19
McKinley, William, 14-15, 24, 45, 70
Mint marks, fraudulent, 38-39
"Mona Lisa," 79
Money, mutilated, 47-49
Moran, William Herman, 115-116
Morgenthau, Henry, 116
Mullen, Terence, 21-22
Mutilated money, 47-49

N

Napoleon, counterfeiting authorized by, 29
Narcotics and Dangerous Drugs, Bureau of, 80
National Crime Information Center (NCIC), 105-106
NCIC, 105-106
New York Police Department, 104, 114
Ninger, Emanuel, 17
Ninhydrin fume hood, 99-100
Nixon, Julie, 67
Nixon, Richard M., 67, 120-121
Nixon, Tricia, 67
"Not worth a Continental," 29

O

Old Capitol Prison, 19
Operative, Secret Service, 108
OPI, 76
Organized Crime Strike Force, 102
Oswald, Lee Harvey, 14

P

Paper money, first U.S., 17
Paranoia, 91
Park Police, U.S., 84
Parkland Hospital (Dallas), 13
Passers, counterfeit money, 28
Pinkerton, Allan, 19, 21
Pinkerton Detective Agency, 21

Police, cooperation by, 101-106
Portraits, U.S. currency, 44-45
Presidential automobiles, 74-75
Presidential Protective Division, 67
Presidents, protecting, 24, 69-94
Procedure, Manual of, 65
Protection, Presidential, 24, 69-94
Protective Forces, Office of, 73
Protective Intelligence, Office of (OPI), 76, 93-94

R

Rayburn, Sam, 120
Redemption Division, Treasury, 47, 49
Report of the President's Commission on the Assassination of President John F. Kennedy, 14
Roosevelt, Franklin D., 70-71, 74, 116-117
Roosevelt, Theodore, 24, 60
Rowley, James J., 80, 118-121
Ruby, Jack, 14

S

Savings Bonds, stolen, 103
Schizophrenia, 91
Scotland Yard, 105
Secret Service, origin of the, 16-19
Secret Service, restrictions on, 24
Secret Service badges, 63
Secret Service Training School, 66, 73
Shantz, Phyllis, 84
Sharpe, Josephine, 57
Sherrill, Col. C. O., 83
"Shinplasters," 17
"Sky Marshals," 80
Snyder, John, 118
Social Security cards, 53
Spaman, Guy H., 117-118
Spanish spies, 22-23, 113
Special agents, training of, 59-68
Stamps, bogus tax, 102
Stanley, 89-91
"Sunshine Special" car, 74
Surete, French, 105

T

Taft, William Howard, 61
Tax stamps, counterfeit, 102
Taylor, Arthur, 113
Taylor, Robert, 121
Teapot Dome oil scandals, 25, 115
Technical Security Division, 76-77
Texas School Book Depository, 14
Threats, death, 88-94
Three Musketeers, The, 101

Torresola, Griselio, 81-83
Trade Mart, Dallas, 11-12
Training, specialized, 76
Training School, Secret Service, 66, 73
Travel, arrangements for, 78
Treasury Air Security Officers (TASO), 80
"Treasury Demand Notes," 17
Treasury Enforcement Agencies, 64
Treasury Law Enforcement Officers School, 64-65
Treasury seal, 43
Treasury Security Force, 86-87
Tribune, Chicago, 112
Truman, Harry S., 71, 74, 118, 121
Tyrrell, Patrick, 21-22

U

Undercover agents, 32-36
"United Commercial Bank, The," 16
United Nations anniversary, 104
United Nations Charter, 79
United States Banknote Company, 68
"United States Notes," 17

V

"VDB," initials on coin, 38

W

Walker, Joseph, 62
Ware, Mrs. Ella, 56-58
Warren, Earl, 14
Warren Report, The, 14
Washburn, Elmer, 108-109
Washington, George, 45
Washington Police Department, 83
Webster, Robert, 60
White House, 18, 81-82
White House Division, EPS, 85
White House Police Force, 81, 83
Whitley, Herman C., 107-108
Wilhelmina, Queen, 116
Wilkie, John E., 112-113
Wilson, Frank J., 116-117, 120
Wilson, Woodrow, 24, 102, 114
Wood, William P., 19, 107
World, New York, 25
World War I, 24

Y

Yarborough, Sen. Ralph W., 11
Youngblood, Rufus W., 11-12

Z

Zangara, Giuseppe, 70-71